unlimited freedom

here is your free audio book

Thank you for taking the time to read this book.
I'd like to send you the audio version 100% free.

Go to: www.fabimarkl.com/freeaudiobook

read this first!

Everything that you're going to read on the following pages is based on my own experience and experiments with the Truth.

There may be some parts that disturb your worldview and contradict your fundamental beliefs. If that makes you angry, the book will help you transform your anger and hatred into love and peace.

If you're still angry after you've read the book, please don't express your anger in the form of physical violence, a death threat or a hate letter. I encourage you to send me an email with your concern to fm@fabimarkl.com

I always set time aside each week for engaging with my readers. I'll even give you a full refund if that would soothe your pain.

Please understand that this book is not intended as a substitute for consultation with a licensed medical, educational, legal or accounting professional. Before you begin any change in your lifestyle in any way, you should consult a licensed professional to ensure that you are doing what's best for your situation.

The use of this book implies your acceptance of this disclaimer.

Have fun ;-)

unlimited freedom

remain calm and at peace no matter what is happening in the world

YOUR GUIDE TO AN AWAKENED LIFE

FABIAN MARKL

It is not location independence that is
freedom, it is freedom that is
location independent.

- *Fabian*

To every single human being on earth:
I'm so grateful that we share this moment together...

conversations

hello.

What if we have met before
in an earlier life?

- *Fabian*

hello.

In The Prophet Kahlil Gibran writes, "When you are born, your work is placed in your heart."

At the end of April 2014, I graduated from one of the best universities in my country with a dream grade. I should have been celebrating the day I received my Master's degree in Physics, but I couldn't. Why? Because I suddenly realized that this was not the work that had been "placed in my heart."

So, I left my "promising" career path that I had been working so hard for over the past seven years and moved back into the basement of my parents' house. It's true, there were moments when I felt like a failure. Although I was approaching 30, I was still living at home and dependent on my parents' money.

But there are three things that I have been certain about for my whole life. First, I always need a second chance. Second, I never give up. Third, I always found a deep love and joy in reading. I read over 120 books that year - 10 books a month.

Over a period of four months, I would sit down each morning and write out two pages from Paulo Coelho's The Alchemist by hand. One day, I wrote down three lines that would change the course of my life forever:

As he [the boy] was about to climb yet another dune, his heart whispered, "Be aware of the place where you are brought to tears. That's where I am, and that's where your treasure is."

That night, I imagined holding a book in my hand that had my name on it. I noticed a tear of incredible joy running down my cheek. The next morning I started to learn and practice the art of writing. For weeks, I had no idea what the book I would write was about.

In the summer of 2015, I took all the notebooks and folders that I had been filling with stories, quotes, life lessons, ideas, observations about human nature and my own self-talk for the past five years, and started to organize them into similar topics.

I withdrew from my social life and dug deeply into this process and something started to take shape. I had not only found my own writing voice and style, but I also found a short piece I had written about a moment in 2013 when I had experienced a profound inner transformation:

For years, I had a regular German student's life, but I was living in intense anxiety. I thought I would die each time I left the house, go to sleep, drive a car, walk over a bridge.

For seven months I had been cycling weekly to the 1000-plus-year-old ruined Schauenburg Castle in northwestern Germany located on top of an abandoned stone pit. It was the only place where I could escape the dreadful thoughts.

On December 5th, 2013, on the path, I had an awakening - just one month before my 28th birthday.

As always, about five minutes from my apartment, I had to stop my bicycle in front of a red traffic light. I looked into the red light. I looked at the cars. I looked at the people standing at the crossroads. Then I felt something strange.

"What is controlling these people? Who is really telling them which way to go? Do they have a choice, right at this moment, to change their direction?" This thought

started to silently loop into my mind. "It is the voice in their head." "It's very likely," I thought, "that I am the only one here at the crossroads who knows that."

My mind went blank. All my thoughts were gone. I was completely immersed with the present moment. Everything moved in slow motion. A chill was running over my body. It felt as if I had stepped into an anthill and millions of ants were crawling over my skin. I got goosebumps.

I instantly knew that my life would never be the same again. I felt that the old species inside me had just died, while a new species was awakened. Tears shot into my eyes.

The lights turned green and I continued my journey towards the castle ruin. As I reached the top, the wind started to blow hard and it seemed as if the trees were celebrating my arrival. I leaned the bicycle against a bench and took out my smartphone. I opened the voice recorder and began to speak:

"If I can be aware of the voice in my head, then I am not the voice! But, if I am not the voice, then who am I really?"

After I returned to my apartment, I took out a pen and a little notebook and started to write down what became the basis for this book.

Reading that again ignited a spark inside me that this would be my Life's Task - to show every human being on earth that, no matter how old you are, what body you have, or what your life situation is, there is a way to live without unhappiness, suffering, stress and fear. That's what I call "awakened life". And the best thing about the awakened life is that it's available to you now - right at this moment.

Over the next few months, I observed myself and the world through the eyes of a person who lives free from the voice in the head. Then I imagined a person in a certain life situation coming to me and asking me simple questions. All I did was writing down the answers.

For most of you, the journey to creating peace and freedom inside is going to happen while a busy outside life is challenging you. That's why we will start in part 1 with examining "your peace" and in part 2 slowly move outward to look at "world peace" in the larger sense.

Part 3 brings both parts together and gives you a portrait of a person who lives the principles of unlimited freedom as this is "your next step" in your evolution as a human being.

This book is not just declaring a new philosophy for humanity, but it is encouraging you to move forward with it.

That's how the first milestone of my Life's Task emerged in the form of my first book, unlimited freedom.

It was placed in my heart when I was born - for you.

Sending you all my love
on December 5th 2015,
Fabian Markl

part 1

your peace

"Who am I when I am dead?"
That question is the answer to
who you are while you're alive.

- *Fabian*

freedom from "freedom"

How can I be free? I'm in a wheelchair. I'm in a prison cell. I am in a cubicle. I'm in the basement of my parents' house. Don't you see!?

Given your current circumstances, you may find the phrase "unlimited freedom" quite unrealistic or even disturbing.

You are right. On the external level, your freedom may seem quite limited. But on the essential level, your freedom is unlimited. The purpose of this book is to guide you to that place.

What is "unlimited freedom"?

When you push the clutch in a car, you disconnect the engine from the gear. Then, no matter how far you push the gas, the car doesn't move.

Unlimited freedom is when you disconnect your inner state from the world outside and reconnect it with the world inside. You can push the clutch very easily when you take a conscious breath.

If you take a conscious breath now, your mind is going to be silent. This is who you are. Not the voice in your head. The continuous breathing, in and out, in and out, is guided by your formless infinity not your form identity. Without doing anything, you are always connected to that infinity.

Whenever you reach the ∞ symbol, I suggest you reconnect with the infinite source within you by taking one conscious breath. Bring all your attention to your lips. Notice the feeling that the air produces as it softly touches your lips. To practice, let's take this one breath together now.

Your body is the guardian of the present moment and by bringing all your attention to it, it will let you enter it.

Your inner state is only affected by what's happening in the outside world, when there is an entity that labels, judges and interprets the content of the present moment.

That entity is the voice in your head. When this voice is silent, you are free.

What is my natural state of being?

We travel many miles and climb mountains to see it. Then we sit there looking in awe as the orange disk turns red while it is falling down the horizon.

No matter where in the world we watch a sunset, it makes us feel alive inside, because our heads become silent. That is our natural state of being. I also call it "sunset state".

It's the state where all your problems cease to exist, because your problems are just thoughts that are baked from the batter of your mind.

Isn't meditation the technique I should use to reach that state? Why bother reading or listening to you?

Look around you. Some of the people who are most stressed will tell you that they meditate every day for 10 minutes. The best meditation practice in the morning won't help you awaken inside if you spend the rest of your day outside that state.

Once the Truth inside you recognized itself in this book, you will no longer need meditation to enter the sunset state. You've become the sunset state.

How long does it take me to reach that state? Will I have it after I've read this book?

You don't really need this book to reach that state. This book is just your companion that walks besides you through your life to remind you that this state is available to you in any situation.

You can read this book, look at a sunset, meditate, go to a retreat, or listen to a talk. But you can experience *unlimited freedom* only now.

Place the book beside your bed and you will sleep better. Carry it around with you in your daily life and it will liberate you in some situations.

Will this book help me become who I am?

Good question. If by "becoming" you mean that you have a person in your mind with certain characteristics that you want to be like in the future, then this book will not help you with that.

You cannot "become" who you are, you can only "be" who you are. "Becoming" implies time, while "being" who you are requires no time. You can be who you are only now.

Why is there so much space in the book?

It's not the bite that reduces the hunger, but thespace between the bites. It's not the workout that grows your muscles, but the space between the workouts. It's not the notes that make the music, but the space between the notes. It's the space between two people that makes up the relationship.

It's the space between two thoughts that makes up your essence. It's not the words that accelerate your awakening, but the space between the words. That space makes all the difference.

Are you telling me the truth?

No word you ever hear or read is true. Even the word "Truth" is not true, but a pointer towards the essence that can't be labeled. Don't look at the letters for truth, but at their resonance with the Truth inside of you.

That resonance is experienced in "Aha moments".

What if I have to cry while reading this book?

Be aware of these places where you are brought to tears, because that is when you know you've stepped up to the next rung on your ladder of liberation.

These are the tears of freedom and they will save the world.

∞

freedom from "awakening"

How can I be free? I need to awaken first. Don't you see!?

You've made "awakening", "enlightenment" or "salvation" into a goal or achievement in the future, haven't you? But you can't put it on your bucket list.

Spiritual awakening is not bound to time and is not a superhuman achievement reserved only for the chosen ones.

After all these years. After all these books, retreats, meditations, prayers, I am still not "awakened." What am I doing wrong? I should be awake by now.

You have started to meditate, to pray, to practice yoga, joined a religion, became a follower of a guru, the disciple of a spiritual teacher, you traveled to India or moved into a cabin on a mountaintop. But no one, no book, no practice, no place can bring the "awake" state to you. At best they take things away from you and remind you that what you are searching for is available to you at this moment.

Since I was nine years old, I searched for the absolute truth in this universe. After becoming a physicist, I realized that this truth had been there inside myself all my life.

How does an "awakened life" look like?

“lucid dreaming” is when you become aware inside a dream that you are dreaming. Then you are aware that you could do anything, and that all your doubts and fears are an illusion.

You realize that the only thing that is of absolute importance in that dream is to stay “awake”. You also know that you can’t take anything with you.

The “awakened life” is like “lucid living” where you realize that the dream is, in fact, your life. This is the end of all your suffering, and you get fulfillment just from staying “awake”.

In the awakened life it’s much easier to discover and follow the work you were born to do. And you allow the universe to use you as a flute to gently raise humanity out of its deep slumber.

What is the "deep slumber of humanity"?

The deep slumber is the identification with the voice in your head.

At first, when you realize that who you are is separate from the voice in your head, it may occur to you that you have become insane. The people around you may start to think that, too.

As you advance on your new path, you notice that you have, in fact, stepped out of the insanity, because most things that are considered "normal" in this world reflect insanity. Thus, by having become abnormal, you have become sane.

Help! Nobody in my family is awakened yet. They get uncomfortable and I get frustrated when I talk about it. Should I tell them or pretend that nothing has happened to me?

You might feel in the beginning, that being "awakened" makes you separate from everyone around you. The opposite is true. As an awakened human you can sense your essence and feel the connectedness to every human you meet, awakened or not. Everyone is on their own path of awakening;

if you try to wake them up through force, they will slap you in the face.

Don't point your finger at their conditioned unconscious pattern, but use it to accelerate your awakening. You'll find more guidance in this book.

Is "awakening" the ultimate purpose of my existence?

Yes. There are only two human states: 0 and 1. 0 is the unconscious state, called "asleep". 1 is the conscious state, called "awake". Moving from 0 to 1 is the ultimate purpose of your existence.

Most people have given so much meaning to external things, that they have no meaning left for themselves. Then they spend their whole existence in search of the lost meaning.

At this point, your search is over, because the most significant thing you can find in your lifetime is the true answer to "Who am I?"

∞

freedom from "Who am I?"

How can I be free? I don't know who I am. I have no purpose. Don't you see!?

No matter how often or how deeply you look into the mirror and ask, "Who am I?" or "What is my purpose?" you will never get a true answer. It's not that the questions are wrong, it's the expectation that is. You expect thoughts to arise in your mind that give you the answers. But thoughts are never enough to describe who you are or your purpose.

First, ask the question, "Who am I?" But this time don't answer it with your mind. Let stillness answer it. You will find no answer, and that is the answer. Who you are is not your past story or your body, even though that's what you may still believe.

Who you are is a state of Being that requires no answer or definition by thought. Just by being present, you are who you are and that is when you've fulfilled your ultimate purpose.

Because the answer to "Who am I?" is also the answer to "What is my purpose?"

Isn't my name my identity?

Remember the cubbies in your kindergarten and first school years?

There is a hook in the cubbies with your name on it. Your friends, family, spouse, society, colleagues, media, and government put their stuff on your hook and tell you, "This is who you are. This is your identity."

The "I" in nearly all human interactions points to their identity. You could say the "I" is the abbreviation for "Identity." Or, the "I" is the finger that points to the hook on your cubbies. The words "me" and "my" represent the hook on the cubbies.

On a gravestone, the "I" becomes the dash "-" between the year of birth and death. It tells you how long this name has been on the cubby.

So many things have been put on your hook. What if someone replaced the name on your hook with a number? How would you feel? If you think your name is who you are, a number will cause you to have an identity crisis.

How can your name be your identity, when there are millions of other people who have the same name put upon them, yet they seem completely different from you?

Actually, they are not that much different from you, just what's on their hook is different. Beyond the hook there is nothing that separates you from them.

All hooks are nailed to the same board.

I am my name. I am my job. I am my money. I am my house. I am my family. I am my body. Isn't that who I am?

Nothing in this universe is what it is named. Your name is not your eternal name.

Now, you lose your job. You lose all your money. You lose your house. You lose your family. Then someone takes your name away. Who are you when the hook on your cubby is suddenly empty? When there is nothing left but your body?

Most people will say, "I have nothing any more. I don't know who I am any more. I don't want to live any more."

But we take even these thoughts away from you. No more thoughts in your head. Then we take your body away. Who are you when all forms are lost?

When all forms are lost, everything that remains is the "I am," and that is your eternal name.

Why is knowing who I am so important?

Once you know who you are, you come to your senses.

What before was dead, is now alive.

What before you judged, you now observe.

Where before you were loud, now you are silent.

Where before you reacted, now you are peaceful.

Where before you resisted, now you accept.

Where before you had hate, now you have compassion.

Where before you resented, now you forgive.

Where before there was darkness, now there is light.

Where before you wished for a better past and hoped for a better future, now you enjoy the present.

Where before your life was full of problems, now it is full of this moment.

Is knowing who I am the greatest treasure in this world?

Yes. Some treasures are guarded by the ocean, some by the earth. The greatest treasure in the world is, however, guarded by the Now. But that's where most people never look, and hence will never find it.

It is the ocean in which the thought arises. It is the paper on which the words appear. It is the consciousness that is obscured by the mind.

It is who you are.

∞

freedom from "I am a mother."

How can I be free? I am a mother. Don't you see!?

An actress has to identify herself with a role to play it well. After the scene is recorded, the actress drops the role, because she knows it's not who she is.

When you identify with a function, it becomes a role. Then, you can't see that who you are is not the role.

The most common roles people play are that of a mother, father, housewife, or husband. Even being man or woman are played in roles. Each role comes with a script that gives you standards that your behavior should meet.

When you identify with a role, you identify with arbitrary standards and take each violation as your personal fault. That's when you feel guilty.

What is my function as mother?

Most human beings who give birth to a child fail to make the disidentification with the role they play, and seek out other children for whom they can sustain their role as mother once their own children have grown up.

If you identify with being a mother, this role will trap you and cause you suffering when the child decides to leave you. Since your child does not belong to you, there is nothing you can do.

The child doesn't have to call you every week. Your child may do that on his or her own. Your child offers you this step so you can discover your true essence behind the mother-mask you have been wearing for so long.

Your job in the function of a mother is to prepare your child for this step as best as you can and then let him or her take this step alone. Then you have to step out of the function of being a mother and become who you truly are.

My child screams all the time. I want him (or her) to be still.

You build a room for your child, then you don't give him or her the space to play. When he or she screams you shout, so that the child will be still.

How can the child be still, when you are loud? His or her mouth may become silent, but the child's mind still echoes your scream.

If you want your child to be truly still, you have to become the space for his or her scream. Then your stillness will flow into your child.

I don't know what the child needs. Nobody told me how to be a mother. What should I do?

All the child ever wants is your attention and to feel your presence. Then, you will know what he or she needs. You don't have to know it in your head, you'll know it in your heart. Trust your heart, it has all the answers.

You ask it for guidance not through words, but through your stillness.

I still don't get it. What is the difference between playing a role and fulfilling a function?

A function is like the chair of the boss of a company. Even if you are the boss you don't own that chair. The chair is not a part of you.

You are allowed to sit in that position as long as

you fulfill the function of boss of the company. But once you get fired or retire, someone else will sit in that chair.

When you realize that you are not the chair, you can get up when the time has come.

∞

freedom from "love"

How can I be free? I haven't found true love yet. Don't you see!?

The issue is not that you haven't found it yet. It's that you don't know what true love is.

What is true love?

All people are like clouds. The clouds are different every day, but what's behind the clouds is always the same. If you can see the sun behind the clouds, you know what true love is.

Then, what does "falling in love" really mean?

To most human beings "falling in love" is when their stories, and their bodies, get attached to each other. That's why it's called "attachment love", "romantic love" or simply "love". This "love" may be important for the survival of a newborn, but it becomes a prison for adults.

True love is simpler. For that love, "falling in love" is when you recognize that essence behind someone's surface. It's when "I love you" no longer means "I want you", but "I see my vast essence in you".

Look On Vast Essence, LOVE.

Why do so many marriages end in divorce these days?

Because they lack the foundation of true love. Often the partners in a marriage set up mental rules that must be met if the partner wants to get love.

"If you do this to me, I won't love you anymore. As long as you do that to me, I will love you. Please sign here," one partner says.

True love is unconditional. That's why true love is eternal and "love" can never be eternal.

Why does love sickness feel so painful?

The degree of identification of one partner with the other determines the hole that he or she feels after the breakup. Then people make this hole part of their identity and fill it with ice cream, tears, alcohol, anger and resentment.

That is what love sickness really is: loss of identity. Suddenly, from one moment to the next, you don't know who you are anymore without the other person. That's why it feels so painful.

Love sickness is a sign that you've lost a large part of your identity. Don't try to repair your identity, but leave that space open so that true love can enter. It will not enter from the outside, but from the inside. It's already there.

How do I know that I've found true love?

You can't find it in a person. First you have to recognize it in yourself. Then the love that is in you can recognize itself in another human being.

Or you'll know it after the breakup. When hate arises, it was not true love. Because the opposite of true love is not hate. There is no opposite.

How can I love someone who stole from me, betrayed me, abused me, killed my family?

If you look at a person as if it were a tree, without labeling or judging it, you separate the story that you have about them and the behavior that they show to you in the form of their words or reactions, from their essence. That is true forgiveness.

I am not here to tell you what to do, but to tell you that nobody is able to act beyond their state of consciousness. If a sleepwalker slaps you in the face, you can't make him responsible for that. You were just in the wrong place at the wrong time.

The heavy story with that person charges your body with anger. Without the story, your body will be charged with love.

The choice is yours.

I have hundreds of friends. How do I know which are the true friends?

Technology makes it very easy for us to believe that we can increase our self-worth by adding hundreds of friends to our public self-image, like our social media profile. Your inner narrator wants other inner narrators to believe that you have lot of friends so that you are seen as a "liked" person.

A true friend is a human being who knows you beyond the form in which you appear. This friend doesn't judge your behavior and you don't need to justify your actions.

A true friend is able to distinguish between what is your unconscious pattern and what is your true nature.

Around such a true friend, you naturally drop your outer shell and live out your childlike spirit. You celebrate your true nature together.

The German word for friend, "Freund", is derived from an ancient word that means "loved one". Friends love you as you are and you love them as they are.

When you look at the list of friends you have accumulated over the years, you'll notice that your "best" friends are the only true friends on that list, because they know you on a deeper level. That's why you can communicate with them without words.

This often is just one person. Or you'll find that you have no true friend at all. Then your first step is to be your own true friend. Only once you are your own true friend, will you find true friends.

What's the ultimate gift that I can give on Christmas this year that will express my true love for a person?

Gift giving is one of the more harmless manifestations of the collective obsession with "love". A billion-dollar industry is built upon that story of "love". The intensity of this obsession peaks once a year, on Christmas.

Before that, the script for people's inner narrator is filled with cunning marketing stories that promise the new trend for a present. People start a crazy race to find the present that will make their loved one most happy this year.

No matter what their narrator tells them to buy, they're still anxious about whether it's the right one. You fear that if you don't give a present, the other person may not love you anymore.

What is the ultimate gift you could give a human being whose survival needs like food, water, and shelter are already fulfilled? What is the one thing that the person will always accept and never forget?

Presents are lost, presence is not. Give people your full attention. Do it always. Don't wait for Christmas.

∞

freedom from the "perfect body"

How can I be free? I have to lose weight and build muscles first. Don't you see!?

In our world where the collective mind has become mad, we equal "body" with "beauty".

No matter how big you are, you are a beautiful being. It's your natural state of being. Your beauty cannot be separated from you through the fat or muscles on your body. Your beauty and you are one.

Just look at a Buddha statue; he has a big belly. Still he is a beautiful being, because he has not erected barriers that prevent his true nature from shining through.

See beauty in big Buddha and you've not only got the essence of Buddhism, but the essence of you.

Won't losing weight or building muscle make me more perfect?

No. Your body is not an obstacle to perfection. You become perfect when you become present, because that is who you are.

The "perfect body" can become a futile story that distorts a person's reality entirely. The more that person tries to match his or her mental image with the image in the mirror, the farther the mental image is moving away from the image in the mirror, like a dog that chases its tail.

With every cycle in which the dog fails to reach its tail, it thinks more negatively. It will not take long before the mind of the dog has created a vicious cycle of negative thinking. Then, the dog starts to believe that the only way to escape that cycle is through dissolving the body - committing suicide.

Luckily, dogs don't have a mind, hence don't kill themselves.

So is the key to accept that my body is "imperfect"?

No. "Imperfect" is another story in your head.

You draw a full circle and call it "perfect". Then you put a dot into that circle and you call the circle "imperfect". Now, you look at the circle with the dot and call that "perfect". Then you erase the dot and you call this circle "imperfect".

Can you see the insanity that is induced by both words?

Just because a word exists in the language doesn't mean it makes sense to use it. There are words that make no sense whatsoever. "Perfection" and "Imperfection" are two examples of that kind.

There is, however, one case where it makes sense to use it: only the presence is perfect. It's always in you, hence you can't be imperfect.

You can only be imperfect in the eyes of the world, because these eyes have a blindspot.

I have have always struggled with my weight since puberty. Why is that?

The mind seeks identification with the body. It doesn't care whether the body is healthy, or not. What is considered by a person as a "perfect body" is determined, completely arbitrarily, by the collective story.

In some cultures, an overweight body is seen as beautiful or even healthy, while in others it is considered as ugly and even labeled as a sickness, such as "obesity".

If in the collective mind "being overweight" is regarded as ugly, unhealthy, lazy, or stupid, and if a person who is completely identified with their body becomes overweight, he or she will think "I have become a less valuable person." Then that person tries to repair his or her self-worth through desperation, depression, a feeling of being a victim, taking on new magic powders, fat-loss pills, and fitness programs.

Once the mind has identified itself deeply with "being a fat person", none of these approaches will work in the long-term. The person may lose some weight, but the mind wants to keep its identity alive. Unless you dissolve the mind's intervention in your body change, you will always fall back on the place you started and the mind will keep you in the vicious cycle of failure.

How can I finally lose it?

There are only two ways for permanent change towards a healthier weight.

One is to shift the self-image, and gradually adopt a new identity like "being a person who exercises". This can be done through integrating small movements like one pushup a day or one 5-minute walk a day into your daily routine. Over time you gradually increase the volume or intensity of the movements.

The second is a transformation of your body. But to lose 100 pounds of fat or gain 40 pounds of muscle doesn't mean you've transformed your body. It means you have changed the form of it.

"Transformation" is when you're no longer identified with your body, but have transcended it. This doesn't mean you move out of your body, but deeper into it. You bring more attention to it.

Then you will start eating more real food, and do physical movements that are aligned with your individual nature.

For permanent body change, which of these ways you choose won't matter. For permanent change of the world for the better, undertake the latter approach: Transformation.

Can working out in the gym be a spiritual practice?

Yes. Once you start to go to the gym not to enhance the story that your body tells the world, but to become present in the Now, working out becomes a spiritual practice and effortless.

∞

freedom from food

How can I be free? I need to be a vegan to save the world. Don't you see!?

Meat eaters, vegetarians, paleos, ovo-lactos, fruitarians, vegans; who makes the world a better place?

It depends on how you eat, not what you eat. That means, in which state of consciousness you eat.

A vegan who buys and eats his or her food unconsciously, will do the planet more harm than a person who eats his or her steak in full awareness. Of course, the reverse is also true.

There may be moments in your life where you choose to adopt one of these ways of eating. Do it because you love yourself, not because you fear loss of approval from you peers or missing out on a new trend or you want to save the world.

I ate only plants for two years, now I eat meat again, but in few months I may start eating only plants again. If I adopt a new identity each time, like "I am a meat eater", "I am a vegetarian", or "I am a vegan", it would trap me.

It's not who you are. Change your way of eating if you feel you no longer enjoy it.

The key is not to judge who is the better person, but who is more conscious of what he or she is doing and who is enjoying his or her way of eating more. This is how you save the world.

Does every bite need to be ultra healthy?

You can drive around in an old car or a brand new and more robust car. You can get hit by a truck in both cases. There is no guarantee. That's life.

There is, however, a much higher chance of survival in a maintained and more robust car and you'll get back on track faster after you got hit.

You cannot become healthy; you can only be healthy. Even when you are sick, you can still be healthy. You can still eat food that nourishes your body. There is no need to obsess about health.

There is, however, an advantage if you eat as healthy as you can.

How can I stop overeating?

Most people have lost their connection with their body, and only fill the needs of the mind through it. Their body doesn't need more food, but their mind is still hungry.

The way out of overeating: When your mind wants to keep eating, but your body wants to stop, stop eating. Listen to how your body responds to the food you've eaten.

Two out of three people are overweight or obese. How can we solve that problem?

"The value is in the taste," they say.

Eighty percent of the food that you can buy in the supermarket has no value for your body, because it was designed to give value to your mind only. These companies first throw a sling around your head with their story, then they drive a hook through your tongue with their taste.

Along with their product, they sell you a story. "When you eat this, you become a better person."

Then, you are overweight and a person comes and

tells you, "When you exercise like this, you become a better person."

Can you see the madness?

If you are identified with the story in your head, you can easily become frustrated and depressed.

"The global obesity problem" as experts call it, is a collective manifestation of people who live, eat, and work in the unconscious state. That's why it cannot be solved on a collective level and "eat less, exercise more" is not the primary solution to this challenge.

The primary solution is knowing who you are beyond your story and your body.

You are the solution.

What do you mean by eating unconsciously?

Most people eat in an unconscious, dreamlike state. They buy their groceries while thinking of cooking their meal. They cook their meal while thinking of eating it. They eat their meal while thinking of what happens in the world. They wash the dishes while thinking of tomorrow.

They think they're always one step ahead, while in reality, they are always one step behind. One step behind being conscious and just one step away from their ultimate purpose: waking up out of their story.

What is "conscious" or "mindful" eating?

"Conscious" or "mindful" eating doesn't necessarily mean you eat only food that has been labeled as "healthy". All that matters is that the state of consciousness in which you savor the content of your plate is the same state of consciousness in which you savor the rays of the sun when you're lying at the beach.

At the beginning of our food chain there is always a plant. Plants are where the sun stores its rays for us. Whatever you eat, you chew on the sun.

Make every bite shine through you.

∞

freedom from "I don’t know."

How can I be free? I don’t know what to do. Don’t you see!?

Sometimes you don’t know, but still you know.

Twenty years ago I didn’t know I’d write this book, but still I knew I‘d write it.

I didn’t know why I had to move in with my parents at the age of 29, but still I knew.

I didn’t know why I had to write all words in my notebooks in English, but still I knew.

I didn’t know why I had to study the art of writing, but still I knew.

I knew this book wanted to be born. All I knew was that I had to prepare for its birth.

Should I ask my family for guidance?

"You are a [enter your family name] and we have always been businessmen," your family tells you.

If you feel that inner knowing that you are an artist, you may face resistance from the inside and outside. Inside you identify yourself as a member of the family. On the outside the members of your family identify themselves with you.

"I am your mother, father, brother, sister, uncle, aunt, grandfather, grandparent", they say and use those labels to describe the roles they play.

Their expectation becomes a part of your identity. As a child they always touch your head and say, "You are going to become a great businessman and continue the family business." You start to make that a part of your story.

As you graduate from school, you enroll in an university program that teaches you everything you need to know about business. After seven years of studying, you're just few months away from your graduation when you suddenly realize that for all these years, you've been living a lie.

Since you were a child, you have always known on a deep level that you are not a businessman. You've always felt a slight headwind blowing you in a different direction, but you pushed along the story that your family had written for you. Finally, you fall into a crisis.

You don’t know what you should do. You don’t know who you are anymore. You don’t know whether you should finish your studies at all. You just have to finish your final thesis, but now you feel huge internal resistance towards ever writing another word of it. You call your parents.

"I don’t know if I want to finish this," you tell them.

"Finish what?" your mother answers.

"My studies!" you respond.

"Why not? We've invested $80,000 and you have invested many years in it," she says.

"It doesn’t matter anymore. I realized that I don’t want to become a businessman," you tell her.

"You don’t have to become one. You can finish this, and then do what you really want to do," she assures you.

"But it has nothing to do with business," you say.

"Maybe you're right. You may never need what you've studied, but you never know. One day you will be grateful that you finished it. Everything in the universe is connected in some magical way," she tells you.

"So what should I do?" you ask.

"Finish your thesis. Do it in a state of gratitude. Because it will be your last act in this field." She responds.

"Okay, thanks," you say, hang up and finish your studies.

Sometimes, it may be wise to ask your family for advice to assure you of what you already knew.

Is my family my true guidance?

The most important relationship in your life is with the Now, not your family.

That relationship alone determines the quality of your entire life.

The Now is your true guidance, not your family.

I feel lost, as if I had fallen off a ship in the middle of the ocean and now I could swim in any direction. I can't see land on any side. I don't know which way to swim.

The source of all things is the water in the ocean. Everything you will ever get in your life is already in this ocean. When you're born, you enter that ocean and start to swim.

"Focus on the things that float within your reach and get there as fast as possible," the people close to you suggest.

You reach the first thing, but you're stressed, exhausted and tired. You can't really enjoy the thing you've reached, because you feel it is not yours.

As the things you get bring you no joy, you think that the reason you feel bad is because you don't have this bigger thing over there.

"If I could add this thing to my life, then I will be happy," you tell yourself.

You swim as fast as you can towards the next thing you can see with your eyes, because you don't trust your heart.

With every new thing you reach, however, you feel worse.

"There must be something wrong with me," you start to think.

Then suddenly you reach the other side of the ocean. Your life is over and you wonder why you didn't enjoy it even though you reached so many things. You feel your life has been wrong.

There is, however, a different approach. You swim, not guided by what you see or hear outside, but what you see and hear inside.

Now, your directions are set by your intuition. If what you see with your eyes will lead you into a direction that doesn't feel right, you swim past it without giving it another thought, because you trust in the guidance of your heart.

You don't actually have to swim, because something does the swimming for you. All you do is enjoy being a part of this ocean. You feel the connection with everyone and everything that shares this water with you.

It may take longer for you to reach a thing than it

takes for other swimmers, but it doesn't matter, because you'll reach your thing in a joyful state and be more peaceful with it.

You continue your journey without holding onto the things you get, because you know taking them with you would make it harder to swim, drown you and once you reach the other side, you won't need them anyhow.

Some days the wind is blowing hard and the waves are high. You can barely keep your head afloat, and you feel you go in circle, when you look at the sky. To the eye the ocean seems dark, but inside yourself you can always see the spark.

All you need to dissolve the fear that blocks the action is to become free from "I don't know". That is to trust in your inner guidance even if it leads you into darkness - especially then.

The outside world may be completely uncertain to your head. Yet, still, inside, the voice in your heart gives you certainty. It's time to trust in that.

Your heart offers you courage in exchange for knowledge.

That's all you need to know.

∞

freedom from the world

How can I be free? I have to react to this situation. Don't you see!?

A reaction is a conditioned way of responding to the world. It's a rejection of the present moment.

You are sitting in your garden in the grass with your family for dinner. It's summer, warm, and some wasps are circling around the delicious food on the table. You can't stand these wasps. And you use your whole body to get rid of the wasps.

You observe your son. A wasp lands on his finger. He observes it. He studies it. He does nothing about it.

Then your son looks at you and asks you, "What is your story about wasps?"

"I have been conditioned to believe that they want to sting me," you answer.

"Interesting", he says. "I have been conditioned to believe that they are in search of food for their offspring and themselves. Can you see how they look on my finger for food, but don't sting me?"

"That is crazy. Their way of flying looks so aggressive. In the news they write about them as pests, " you respond.

"Maybe you should ask what the wasp's story about you is," he suggests.

"Okay, wasp. What is your story about me?" you ask.

"I have been conditioned to believe that you prepare delicious food and that I have to sting only when my life is threatened. My target is the food, not you," your son responds.

You will still experience the urge to react whenever a wasp lands on your plate, but now you have a choice, to create space around your action by observing the real intention of the wasp and not interfering with it, but being with it.

You don't have to smash the wasps; but give them just gentle signs that this is your food. Or better, put your leftovers on a separate plate where the wasps can nourish themselves and are not disturbed.

You'll see how peaceful the wasps munch and realize that they made you a more peaceful person.

How can I become non-reactive?

You become reactive only when you judge, interpret on the basis of your past conditioning, which is your story.

Your perception determines your reaction if you're not conscious of it. Your perception is derived from what you think is the intention of the other person.

Whenever there is no space between your perception and action, you act out of that conditioning.

Non-judgment is when you separate your story and other people's behavior from who they are.

But sometimes I have no choice to react differently.

Really?

It's another mad morning.

You just finished your coffee. Now, you look for your car keys, but you can't find them at the place where they usually are. You look in your jacket, but still, you can't find them.

"Did you use the car yesterday?" you ask your spouse.

"Yes," your spouse says.

"Where did you put the keys then?" you reply.

"I think I left them in the car," your spouse tells you.

You go to the car and look, but the car is locked. You look at your watch and a negative emotion starts to take form in your body.

"You make me mad. Why can't you put the car keys where they always are? Now I have to take the spare keys, because of that," you tell your spouse.

"I am going to be 5 minutes late to work. What a shame!" you say to yourself.

While you're driving, you think about the incident all the time. You feel stressed because you come to work a few minutes late. You arrive in a negative mood. You tell all your colleagues what happened to justify your negative mood.

You tell yourself the story of what happened throughout the day. Your mind recycles it until it becomes another part of your identity.

"My spouse always does that," your inner narrator tells you.

You arrive at home in the same negative mood as you left. You couldn't escape the trap of negative thinking. You just reacted to your environment, completely unconscious of the present moment.

You think you had no choice to react differently. That's what the narrator wants you to believe. In fact, you could have reacted kindly and lovingly. All this would have taken is to become aware of the emotions you were experiencing, accepting them, and then creating space around them. Instead of rushing out the door, you could have sat down for 10 seconds and taken three conscious breaths.

The most important thing is not the action, but the space in which the action happens. That is what determines the quality of the action.

If your state of space is peace and compassion, you realize that it was nobody's fault that the keys weren't where they were supposed to be. You knew that today, you were meant to take the spare keys. You were meant to be 5 minutes late.

There have been people who were delayed before you and missed their plane. They sent messages of anger and hatred to the people who "did" that to them. Then their plane crashed in the ocean. No one survived. Then they sent letters of love and gratefulness.

You never know what effect the content of the present moment will have on your life. So, be grateful for everything you get to experience in the Now.

Never reject the present moment, but always align yourself with it. It may save your life one day, and it will save your joy every day.

Where do the emotions behind the reaction come from?

Your story gives all your emotions their taste. Your body doesn't know whether the story is real or fiction and translates it into emotions anyway. Emotions are the mind's means to get you to act on a thought.

Your mind creates the story like "smash that fly" and your body translates it into an emotion. If you observe the fly in wonder, the emotion will subside.

Then, the fly and you have become one.

How can I become free from the world?

An emotion is a story that has taken form in the body. A reactive behavior is an emotion that has taken form in the world.

When you have become free from your story, you have become free from the world.

That is, to accept this moment as if you had chosen it.

∞

freedom from technology

How can I be free? I got a message, I have to reply. Don't you see!?

If humans remain unconscious, robots will become like humans and humans will become like robots.

Pavlov was a scientist who had a dog, which he conditioned. Whenever he rang a bell, the dog expected food and its mouth started to water. Through smartphones, humans have become like dogs.

The smartphone conditions human behavior very effectively. Once it gives a sound or a vibration, we are pulled to reach for the phone, no matter whether we are cooking, eating, watching TV, driving a car, riding a bicycle, walking across the street or talking to someone.

The phone rings but we cannot not answer it. It could be important, and if it's not important, we resent the caller.

The phone vibrates but we cannot not answer the

text message. We feel compelled to answer within a certain time period, because the sender knows you've read it, and if you don't reply he or she may be disappointed.

Before you grab your smartphone now, ask yourself, "Am I the dog or am I the master?"

How can I be the master?

Today, when someone speaks to you, calls you, or sends you message, wait, listen and observe your response without expressing it. After a while, you may find that the urge to reply has lessened or even ceased.

We reply to people we don't like, because we feel we should, and because it's just one click. A true response is one that you give without expecting an answer in return.

If you give people space for their response, they may even send you a letter. Wouldn't that be beautiful?

Doesn't my smartphone make me "smarter"?

For one week I decided to leave my smartphone switched off.

I looked at some food, but it didn't look so good, even though it was kept in the fridge and was still within date. My body said "No" to eating it instantly. My mind wanted to know whether I could still eat it. So I felt the urge to switch on the smartphone to check whether I could eat the food.

But I listened to my body, and didn't eat that food. Instead, I cooked something that was fresh. Even though the "smart" phone could have told me that I could still eat it, I threw it away. I realized that the smartphone made me lose trust in myself, in my body's signals.

If you no longer trust yourself, who is left to trust? Your body is smarter than your phone.

Isn't it great to capture every moment forever?

You come to a beautiful scene in nature. You take out your camera, but the light isn't right. You can't take a proper picture. You try to adjust the settings, but it still isn't right. You get stressed because other people are waiting to take a picture too.

So you just take one and turn your back towards the scene without even looking at it with your own eyes. You gained a picture, but you lost the moment.

You are used to experiencing the world through a screen. You film and photograph each event in your life. That is fine, but take a look at the scene first and absorb it with all your senses.

Can you see how the bird on the branch looks at you? Can you hear the wind whispering its secrets in your ear? Can you smell the fresh scent of the forest entering your nose? Can you feel the joy of the tree in front of you celebrating your presence?

First enter the moment fully, then if you want, capture it.

∞

freedom from "I am different."

How can I be free? I am different. I have to stand out. Don't you see!?

In a world where everybody wants to stand out, all are the same, and those who will stand out are all themselves.

We sit together at your favorite lake among hundreds of others who enjoy taking a cool bath in the summer heat.

We think we are so different from each other on an external level. Look at how some reinforce their differences through tattoos, haircuts, dresses, and cars. They do not see the truth, that all their efforts are in vain, because on our essential level, we're all the same.

Every movement they make, every word they speak comes from the same formless substance. It may actually come from their minds, but below the mind's surface there is always the formless.

Children, teenagers, mothers, fathers, the old, even

the fishes are connected through the formless and that is timeless.

What would happen or how would the scene here at the lake look if all of these people knew this truth? There would be no barriers to talk to each other, because these barriers are mind-made illusions.

They wouldn't be ashamed to run around naked and others wouldn't be offended. They would smile at each other, never frown. People who smile have become a rare species.

Smile now, and you stand out ;-)

But I just tried to be more authentic. Is that wrong?

Chameleons change their skin color to match it with their environment. In social environments, people are like chameleons whose skin color is their self-image.

People act out a slightly different self-image for every person. They act in the way that they think is the self-image the other person has constructed about them.

When people sense that they are acting out a false self-image, they try to be more authentic, and start to act out another self-image that they're more identified with.

They will never reach a level of full authenticity with any self-image. Only when they have completely disidentified with their self-images, will they be truly authentic.

When only the stories of people interact, it's no wonder that most relationships are inauthentic, even between two people who have been married for 30 years.

Isn't small talk the quick way to connect with other people?

When your story is active in your interaction with someone else, it's likely to interact with the other person's story, and the interaction appears shallow or "small" to you.

Once you interact without a story, the attention that you needed to protect your story becomes available to you.

Then you can put that attention in his or her eyes,

and you will connect with the other person more deeply in a few seconds than you ever could with a shallow conversation that lasted for a decade.

∞

freedom from "I am more than you."

How can I be free? I need to show the world my status. Don't you see!?

"Why is this handbag so expensive? It has the same look and quality of the one that costs half the price," you ask the merchant.

"You pay for the name," she responds.

What does it mean to "pay for a name"?

It means that the value of the name of the company has been branded into the collective unconsciousness through repetitive storytelling as "exclusive".

Marketing experts and advertising professionals call this "unconscious branding". Political experts and government professionals call this "propaganda". They all write the script for the voice in your head.

The expensive brands promise you that whenever

you hold their bag in your hands and walk in public, the bag will tell the world a more valuable story about who you are. Of course, that is all an illusion they sell to you.

It's not bad to buy these brands, but don't add the bag to your identity to enhance your self-worth. If you carry around an empty bag, you know it's really the narrator who bought it.

Then look inside, and that space is you.

Why does my inner narrator tell me to wear clothes that show certain brand names?

Your narrator doesn't like clothes that have no visible name or label on them because it wants your identity to be reinforced by your environment. The name on your clothes is not part of who you are, just a tool for people to tell themselves a story about what your identity may be.

I am in a powerful position, but I don't understand why people don't listen to me. What am I doing wrong?

To touch people, you need to talk from a deeper place, not a higher one.

First, you need to find the deep place within yourself. This means knowing who you are beyond the function you fulfill, beyond your body and your personal history. At that place you and everyone you talk to are one.

Second, whenever you talk to someone you must keep some connection to that deep place. This means you always keep some attention inside the energy field of your body.

Then the words you speak will carry that universal energy vibrations and resonate deeply with the person who receives them.

I always get nervous when I interact with a powerful person. How can I increase my confidence?

Whenever you get nervous when you interact with someone who has created a greater self-image than yours, you feel inferior, even though it's all an illusion created by both of you.

Confidence that is derived from a story that you tell yourself about yourself, and other people tell themselves about you, is false confidence.

True confidence doesn't come from your story of "I

am more than you" or "I believe in myself", but from knowing who you are beyond your story.

When you interact without story, you no longer require confidence. That is your true power.

∞

freedom from "greatness"

How can I be free? I am not "great" yet. Don't you see!?

"Greatness" is a story in the collective head. When you have won that number of titles, then you are great. When you did this that no one ever did before, then you have become a "legend."

If you do anything because you want to be viewed as "great", you will lose.

The word "greatness" has been misused like the words "Love" and "Truth". It has been attached to achievement. True greatness is attached to the infinity of the formlessness that has no boundaries or conditions. Your essence is greatness. You are born out of greatness. You are already great.

Nothing external and no experience needs to be added to you to make you great. There is nothing in this universe that is greater than you, because you are the universe. You are perfect.

Recognizing that is where true greatness comes from.

Do I need people's attention to become great?

Singular attention makes a person important. Collective attention makes a person famous. No attention makes a person great.

I feel I have adopted a vision from someone else, because I don't know what mine is. What now?

The seedling of a tomato plant has the inner vision of becoming a tomato plant.

Then, it sees an orchid standing next to it and decides to become an orchid instead as it's seen as a more beautiful plant in the eyes of the world and people look more at the orchid than at the tomato plant.

The tomato seedling tries very hard to create the new inner vision of being an orchid, but it can never keep it in its imagination for very long. The tomato plant suffers from that and doesn't grow well.

One day, it decides to surrender to its original inner vision. Suddenly the leaves start to spread and it grows faster in size than ever before. It feels aligned with its true nature. It knows that it doesn't do the growing, but it lets the space that surrounds it manifest the inner vision into the world.

Then the first tomato starts to grow and turns red. A child grabs the tomato, bites into it and smiles at the tomato plant. In that moment, the tomato plant knows what its external purpose is: to bring a smile to people's faces through its fruit.

And it realizes the purpose of the orchid next to it: to bring a smile to people's faces through its blossoms.

Whenever a vision requires your effort to hold in your imagination, it's not yours. If the thing you get is not yours, you will feel worse, because you know you've been lying to yourself and the world.

Every living being has the inner purpose to align itself with its own nature and the external purpose to bring a smile to people's faces in its own unique way.

∞

freedom from "work"

How can I be free? I have to create extraordinary work. Don't you see!?

When something is inside of you, at some point it wants to be born. You are the obstetrician.

Extraordinary things come out of you when you're in a state of awareness, rather than conditioned reaction or wanting.

This can take many forms, like words, a smile, a painting, or just playing with your child.

"Extraordinary" doesn't necessarily mean that what you do has the most impact on the world. Some of it will. But more important is how doing it made you feel.

If creating something made you feel extraordinary, then it was extraordinary work. Creating a smile on your face or someone else's face is extraordinary work.

What is the difference between being motivated to do

something and being inspired to do something?

Motivation is derived from the mind's identification with external forms such as status, approval, reputation, money, or pleasure.

To do something you don't want to do requires continuous motivation.

Inspiration is a state of being that emanates from within you as love, joy, enthusiasm, and peace that are aspects of your true nature.

To do something you were called to do requires singular inspiration.

Motivation will get you to the gym. Inspiration will get you to the moon.

What does it mean "to be in love with what you do"?

Identifying yourself with what you do is obsession. Seeing yourself in what you do is passion.

"Am I in love with what I do?" is in reality the question of "am I in love with the present moment?"

Even if you hate your job, you have to accept that this is what the present moment is like for you. Effective change can only come out of acceptance for what is.

Do I need to be intelligent to be creative?

Intelligence is not the opposite of stupidity. Splitting the atom was intelligent, creating the atomic bomb was stupid. IQ tests have nothing to do with intelligence.

Hence, creativity does not depend on your IQ, but on your connection to the present moment and that is when you become one with your doing. Some people call this experience "being in the zone" or "flow".

When you ask them, they often say, "It was as if I did nothing, but it was being done."

That happens when you've become one with the Now and become who you are. You are the channel through which your formless essence can flow through into the world and manifest itself in the form of the work you created. Such work has timeless quality and will forever be admired by generations of people as "not being from this world".

"Work" has become the term to describe the act of manifesting form out of form, like building a house out of bricks or building software out of code. "Work" was once "creation". "Creation" is the act of manifesting form out of the formless.

Only once you are one with the formless can you create form that is timeless. To become one with the formless is to become present and silent. Out of that state you create eternity.

You have been created out of the formless, and thus are eternal. You are not your work, you are the timeless space.

You are the flow. Be that.

∞

freedom from "I am a failure."

How can I be free? All of my friends got married, picked a city, make more money, bought a house and have children. I feel so behind. I am a failure. Don't you see!?

Whether your life is a success or a failure does not depend on whether you've added any of these things to your life. It solely depends on how rusty or shiny your connection is to this moment. That's what humanity needs most.

Why does failure make me feel depressed?

To take one right step, you have to take a thousand wrong steps. No wonder you'll get depressed when you focus on your outcomes.

"On the top of the mountain you will be happy". The world tells you.

Then you reach the top, and are happy for five minutes. Then the world says, "You need to get to a higher mountain to be even happier". You do that. Still, on the higher mountain you're happy for just five minutes.

Once you realize that every step is right, you no longer need to fight.

You will start to float.

Isn't failure the opposite of success?

You select a big mountain as your goal. Then you climb that mountain with all your energy and resources. You are almost there. With all you have left you drag yourself to the top. You feel relieved. The weather and the view are great.

"Yes! I made it. After seven years of hard work, I am at the top," you say to yourself.

You look around and suddenly something catches your eye. Your heart drops to your stomach. You realize that you are on the wrong mountain. Somehow you got sidetracked. That one over there was the one you wanted to climb and it's twice as high!

Now you have two choices. First, you can pretend that this was the mountain you've wanted to climb anyway, because you don't want to tell all your friends and family that you've climbed the wrong mountain.

Second, you can admit to yourself and others that you're on the wrong mountain. You pick up your feet, put your heart back in place, and start walking down to the bottom. Then you take a few breaths and start climbing again, but this time up the right mountain.

You notice that you have more energy and skills than you had for your first mountain. Then at the top of the right mountain, you look back at the previous mountain and realize that it wasn't wrong, but part of the journey.

Without the wrong mountain you wouldn't have had the strength to climb the right and higher one.

Failure is not the opposite of success, but an essential part of it.

What is success?

In our world, "success", still, is a collective story derived from the content of the present moment, like numbers of book sales, TV appearances, or dollars in a bank account. That story is wrapped around the essence of a person. Then this person is labeled as "successful."

We are told that success is getting what you planned to get. But achieving, winning, status, praise, and failure are all mere byproducts of success.

A "Yes" to whatever the content of the present moment is, that is true success.

If it's not success, then what is the secret to happiness?

Pleasure is in the body.

Pleasure is external, because you derive it from something outside of you. Chocolate, sex, Alcohol, drugs, TV.

Happiness is in the mind.

"If I have this, then I am allowed to feel happy. If I have done this, then I am allowed to feel happy. If I am like that, then I am allowed to feel happy."

Enjoyment is in the spirit.

Enjoyment is internal, derived from your essence. And since your essence is always the same, you can derive enjoyment from it anytime and anyplace.

Knowing who you are is the secret.

∞

freedom from "more"

How can I be free? I need to have more than last week. Don't you see!?

Each week you fill the space in your house with more things. The house becomes heavier. The air becomes thinner. You start to worry more, because you are afraid that someone might steal your things. You haven't touched eighty percent of these things in the past four years.

"You may need this soon. There are great memories attached to this shirt," your inner narrator tells you.

You have to get rid of a part of the garden so you can build another house for your 10,000 things. After a year, that house is stuffed too. You can't build another house and you don't want to let go of the things, but still want more. You continue filling even the tiniest spaces.

One day, both buildings collapse under the weight of the things. Then you collapse under the weight of the loss. You have nothing left. You are depressed. You can't jump from the roof, and that makes you even more depressed. You sit there in the remains of your lifelong obsession.

"All is lost!" you start to weep.

Suddenly, you sense something strange. "This tear can't be true," you say to yourself, "it tastes too good."

You get on your feet, and it feels like you are floating. You feel like a butterfly that has just shed its cocoon. You feel liberation.

You decide to build another house, that is half the size, but with twice the space.

Do you think I should become a minimalist?

Don't let the inner narrator trick you into an obsession for letting things go. It can find an identity for you even in that and tells you to become a "minimalist". This may make sense for a certain period of time, but don't look for yourself in it, otherwise it will trap you.

You won't become "less" when you let go of "more". You won't become "more" when you let go of "more".

You will become who you are when you let go of both "less" and "more".

Only when we become free from the mind-made affirmation of "more", will other human beings who have less than is sufficient get more. In the western world, we believe that having more than less is necessary, while the truth is, for us less is more than necessary.

I realized that I am just wearing 8 out of my 40 shirts. Why do we accumulate so many things even though we don't need them? Why is it so hard to let them go?

For most people, existence is a dance between the hunger for "more" and the fear of "loss".

The mind is hungry to add things to your identity to make you more of who you think you are. At the same time, the mind's greatest fear is that you will lose what you have added to yourself, because then you'll lose parts of who you are.

There are only two ways to escape that vicious cycle of "more", that often manifests itself in the form of greed. Don't attach more stuff to your neverfull mind, but spend your money on what gives you meaning, not pleasure.

Or perhaps the better solution: find a way to earn your money in a way that gives you meaning.

The best solution: give what you don't need to those who need it.

Why are people so obsessed with money?

"This piece of paper is as valuable as that piece of gold." That is the whole story of money. "I am as valuable as these pieces of paper." That is the whole story of human obsession with money.

Authorities are the authors of large parts of our stories. They put their heads on a nice piece of paper to make their story more believable. That alone would not be a problem, but people started to identify themselves with that story, and that's when money became dangerous.

Remember, "money" is just a story in the head, nothing real. You doubt that? Look at how easy it is for the authorities to change the story and modify the value of money.

"Now your money is two percent more valuable than yesterday," they say.

That's completely arbitrary. We believe what they say, because they are the authors of our stories.

You think, "more money" is what you want, but the truth is, you want the story that money tells other people about yourself.

Why do I feel that I never have enough?

You are the mother. You buy the groceries for your family. You see your son eating rice, so you buy him four packages of rice. The next day he eats quinoa, hence you buy him four packages of quinoa. Then he eats spaghetti and you buy four packages of spaghetti. The next day, he doesn't eat anymore carbs. Now, you have 12 packages of food that nobody eats.

You were afraid that you didn't have enough, although if you're honest with yourself, you were actually afraid of not being enough of a mother.

The fear of not having enough is in its essence the fear of not being enough. Both fears are false. By having the present moment, you always have more than enough.

You are the present moment. What more can you ask for?

∞

freedom from time & stress

How can I be free? I have no time. Don't you see!?

You are right. You have no time, because "time" is a story in the head, nothing real.

One Second is the story about a certain atom called cesium-133 that has changed its ground state 9 billion times.

For the human mind, time is measured by how often the content of the present moment changes. When there is no change in content, it feels as if time doesn't move fast enough. When there is a lot of change in content, it feels as if time has gone too fast.

The more you want the content of the present moment to be different, the longer it takes for it to change. The more you accept the content of the present moment, the faster it will change.

What causes the most stress in people is the story of time. Stress is a sign that you resist the present moment and want its content to be different.

Then, the story of time in your head turns into stress in the body.

No time, no stress.

Isn't it boring when the content of the present moment doesn't change?

The mind wants new content every three seconds. It can satisfy its desire very easily, by looking at the smartphone for new messages, looking at the newspaper for new stories, looking at the stores for new products, looking at your email inbox for new requests, looking at the TV for new shows.

It offers a way for the mind out of the perceived emptiness of the present moment which it labels as "boredom".

This often occurs when a person is used to constant content change, because he or she has been playing video games that have this characteristic. When the person stops playing, he or she will perceive reality as quite slow compared to the virtual world he or she is used to. This person then feels restless.

For people who feel restless, the emotion of boredom manifests itself in behaviors like biting fingernails, pulling hair out, shaking legs, pulling things out of the nose, or scratching the head.

They think once they allow boredom, they become a "boring person". Who puts that label upon them? It is the mind, not you. Your true nature can never be bored.

Observe the bored mind, like a baby that got bored playing with the same doll.

"I want a new doll!!" the baby screams.

You observe it, but do nothing. Soon you realize that the baby becomes still and peaceful. That's when you have become that baby. Its name is "presence".

Whenever you are bored, call for "presence".

Why do I feel stress when I get stuck in a traffic jam on the way to work?

You drive to work and the present moment contains a "traffic jam". The more time goes by the more you want this content to be "sitting in the chair at your work desk".

The stronger the desire gets, the more stressed you become. That desire is fueled by only one thing: glimpses at your watch.

When you are stuck in traffic, the universe wants you to become present, not to look at your watch. If all people would get this message and drive without a watch, traffic accidents would drop by 99%.

Often, the bruises on your car and body tell your story of time. They are a collection of moments of unawareness.

Is patience the same as presence?

No. Patience is accepting the content of this moment as it is under the condition that it will change in the future. This is where hope arises. Presence is accepting the content of the present moment, independently of what might happen in the future.

How can I eliminate stress from my life?

To eliminate stress from your life, everything you do must become an entry point into the present moment.

When you enter your car, you enter the present moment.

When you enter the forest, you enter the present moment.

When you enter your home, you enter the present moment.

When you enter your bed, you enter the present moment.

When you enter your shower, you enter the present moment.

When you enter a conversation, you enter the present moment.

When food enters your mouth, you enter the present moment.

Then the present moment will enter you.

What happens when time dissolves?

"It seemed as if time had expanded. These four seconds felt like an eternity." People who have faced a life threatening situation will often describe it this way.

That happens when your entire attention becomes one with the present moment. That's when the story of time ceases to exist and the moment becomes eternal.

The content of that moment gets imprinted so vividly into your memory that you carry it with you throughout your life as if you had it in a box where it stays fresh. When you take this memory out of that box in 50 years, it will still smell as fresh as if you had put it there yesterday.

You don't need a life threatening situation to experience that. A walk in the forest can help you enter that deep state. You walk in alert attention, and listen to every sound and movement.

Then, there will be no thought, no mind, no story and what's left is eternity.

Time is a tool. Time is not you.

∞

freedom from age

How can I be free? I am getting older. Don't you see!?

The summer makes the transition into the autumn. The leaves are turning red and are falling down the trees. You don't want the summer to end, because it was the greatest summer of your life.

You walk around the garden and collect the leaves. Then you paint them green and put them back on the tree.

Even though the average daily temperature has dropped by 10 degrees Celsius, you still walk around in your summer clothes. Soon, you catch a cold and feel sick. All because you resisted the change.

That's what happens when people resist the change in their bodies that we call "aging".

Summer is not better than autumn. The earth just appears to be different on the surface, but at the core, it is always the same.

Doesn't age make me a different person?

"You are this age, so you are this kind of person now. People at this age do such and such things. By this birthday you should have acquired such and such things," the world tells you.

The number of your years of age is nothing more than a story created by the person who invented the calendar a few centuries ago.

How many people suffer because they are completely identified with the number of years that has been assigned to them? Millions? Billions?

Do not determine the value of your life by your years, but by the strength of the connection you have to the present moment.

Life is timeless, it can't be measured. Life just is. You are Life.

But they say my generation is like this.

The mind uses age to divide humanity into generations.

"If you are born in this year, you belong to that generation," experts say.

The truth is, there is only one Generation:

All human beings who are connected through the Now - the thing that unites us all.

Doesn't more age make me wiser?

You are in the gym. You see a person with far more muscles than you doing an exercise in a way that is clearly wrong.

Should you tell him or her that he or she performs the exercise in a way that could cause serious injuries? Or should you not tell him or her, because his or her muscles make you think he or she has more experience in the gym than you?

Often people say that you can't give someone life advice who has more life experience than you. By "life experience" they mean the size of this person's story.

You may have more experience in the world of form than people who are younger. You may have more knowledge about certain things, and could give others guidance to avoid some traps in life, but it doesn't necessarily mean that you are wiser than younger people.

It's not the person with the biggest or longest story who is the wisest, but the person who as none.

You are wisest not on the day before you die, but on the day you were born. Then, you had no story.

More age does not equal more wisdom.

How can I slow down my aging process for free?

There are two ways.

First, your body synchronizes with the second hand of your wristwatch. Get rid of your wristwatch and soon you'll appear decades younger.

Second, your body synchronizes with the amount of time you have stored in your head in the form of "past". Let go of your past entirely.

Most of the stars on the sky have died long ago, yet their light is still telling your eyes the story of their past. Enjoy, the light, but your past is dead.

It has no power over you once you shine the light of your presence onto it.

Isn't my birthday a special day?

Today, on the day when I am writing these words, my body is exactly two months away from its 30th birthday.

"You should really arrange a big party and invite all your friends." My inner narrator tells me. "It's your 30th birthday. It's a special birthday. "

Why is this day so special? It's just another day on earth. The significance of that day is a mental story that has been conditioned into my mind by society. The truth is, 30 is not more special than 20, 18, 13, 27 or 8.

There is not a certain day required to raise the level of my well-being. No day in the future will make me feel better. The days are already perfect.

If there is one thing to celebrate, however, it's not the fact that my physical form turns 30 on that day, but that I am spending this day in the present moment.

The day of my 30th birthday is not more special than the other days. There are only three special days in one's life:

The day when you are born.

The day when you wake up.

The day when you return home.

∞

freedom from fear

How can I be free? Fear is necessary. Don't you see!?

You are in a peaceful state at home. You take a blood pressure monitor and put it on your arm. What you read on the screen makes you scream, "Oh my god! 180!"

Now, you feel scared that you will die. You race to your doctor and she gives you medication to reduce your blood pressure. Your doctor tells you that these are just the side effects of a drug you took for a previous illness. You should not worry much, but just keep monitoring your blood pressure.

The next day, you sit at your kitchen table with the blood pressure monitor in front of you. Just looking at it makes you anxious, because your mind made up a story in your head, like "What if it's at 180 again?"

All fears are created by the story in your head. Your brain "learns" them from your environment and certain events.

All emotions that you label as negative like worry, anxiety, nervousness, unease, tension, and dread are manifestations of mind-made fears. If you're not conscious of them, your fears can be so overwhelming that you're too afraid to take a walk, to give a talk, swim in the lake or measure your blood pressure.

Scientists also call these "irrational fears" or "phobias", but they don't realize that all fears are irrational.

The mind nurtures your fears like an embryo. If you're identified with these fears, your fear of life can surpass your fear of death. That is the ultimate prison your mind can build.

I am afraid of fearlessness. Doesn't fear help me to avoid dangerous situations?

No. Avoidance of falling, startling when you hear a loud sounds or spot venomous animals such as spiders, snakes and scorpions force you into presence. These are not fears since they don't make you nervous, anxious or worried. It is just common sense.

It's a response that makes you act in the present moment. You will find that in such situations you actually become fearless and free from all your problems.

A fear is created in your mind about an event in the future that may or may not happen. That story makes you experience the future in the present moment.

That's why you can walk in the woods, but still feel afraid that you may lose your job next week.

But I am afraid to do it, because I am not good at it.

Being afraid to do something, doesn't mean you have no talent in this area. It's very likely the opposite. Your inner narrator fears doing it, because you might enjoy it so much that you won't go back into your old story.

How can I become free of all my fears?

A person's greatest fear is not death, but being forgotten.

People are scared that their story didn't have a lasting impact. That it will not be told over and over again. That in a few generations, their story will be forgotten.

It's true, your form and your story will be forgotten, but the formless essence that you are will remain forever in this universe. You are immortal and that does not depend on how great your story is.

Even the sun will be forgotten, but its formless essence will remain.

Every fear is connected to the fear of death. What you fear is not physical death, but the death of your story.

To become free from all your fears is to come to the realization of who you are: A being that has no story.

If I have no story, then what do I have?

Presence is the tip of your pen in the moment it touches the paper. Written words are the past, the blank parts are the future. Focus on the tip, because that is where the story of your life is being written.

You have no past. You have no future. You have no story. All you have is this moment.

No fears.

∞

freedom from death

How can I be free? I am going to die. Don't you see!?

Get yourself a glass of water. Take a sip and place it in front of you. Look at it.

Where was the water before it filled your glass?

The water in your glass has already flowed millions of miles through mountain streams and human blood vessels.

Julius Caesar, Leonardo Da Vinci or Gandhi may already have taken a sip from the very same water that is in front of you.

Where will it go after it refreshed you?

This water will enter the stream near your house, and then merge with the closest river.

Ultimately, the water flows back into the ocean. From there it will reach the deepest places on earth. Then it will rise back to the surface and evaporate.

From there it starts its journey back into a different glass.

The glass is your body and your story. You are the water that is returning towards the ocean.

No water is ever lost.

Who am I when I am dead? Water!?

Today, scientists have no clue how many times this universe has been recycled. Many believe that the cycle had no beginning and it will have no end.

All forms in the universe, like the stars in the sky, the galaxies, all the planets in the solar system, the earth and all atoms will move back into the formless.

The final state of the universe is a state of full formlessness where no form exists: a giant field of energy. Then, a new big bang, a new universe, new atoms, new stars, new galaxies, new solar systems, new planets, new earths, a new human species.

Even the sun will die and a new sun will be created out of it. The sun we see on our sky has been recycled two times already.

You may not only have been incarnated in many human forms or life forms on this planet, but you may have walked on millions of other planets already. Consciousness, or whatever you call this energy field, has been in every universe. It is the driver of the recycling process.

It's not the universe that expands, it's the consciousness that expands the universe. It expands until all forms are dissolved, then it goes back to a singularity. At this point, there is only presence, because that is where the present moment is born.

Physicists say that "time didn't exist at this point", because there was only presence and time was never born out of the formless, but has been created by the human mind.

The present moment that is in you now, is also the very moment that was present at the birth of the universe. In that way, one could say, when you become conscious of your own presence, you can feel the universe come to life.

"Who am I when I am dead?" That question is the answer to who you are while you are alive.

Is there a chance that I can become immortal?

Lots of people in this world seek to become immortal through the form of their story, their stuff, and by having and doing, but fail to recognize that immortality is only accessible through being, through the formless.

They want to find Heaven after death, blind to the fact that in their final hour, they'll realize that they are Heaven.

Heaven is eternal, the mind is not. The word "Heaven" is a metaphor for the awakened consciousness. Only your form has its beginning at your birth and its end at your death.

It's the ultimate purpose of every human being to sense that immortality while still being in the world of form.

You are immortal, right at this moment.

∞

part 2

world peace

If each of us thinks his or her truth is absolute,
we will become a planet of gravestones.
If each of us thinks his or her truth is relative,
we will become a planet of bright stars.

- *Fabian*

the fault in our stories

What is the fault in my story?

It all started with a single cell, that looked like a chicken egg without the shell.

After nine months in that womb, it was time to leave and someone pulled you out into the world. Everything about you was fresh. Your skin so soft like it will never be again. Your eyes were filled with wonder like never again. Your brain was like a blank notebook.

From that moment onward, until the very moment now as you are reading these lines, your story has been written on that notebook. Who writes the first line on the first page of your notebook? Your parents. What's the first word they write on it? Your name. You have no choice. This is what you will be called for the rest of your life.

Your name becomes the central part of your identity, the belief about who you think you are. That belief is the fault in your story.

Where does the voice in my head come from?

You are born in your essence without a voice in your head. Your umbilical cord will be replaced by a cord from the environment through which your inner narrator is nurtured.

Scientists have identified the area in your brain where the narrator is located. It's called the "cortex". He sits there in your big walnut, in a chair near a fireplace, with the notebook on his lap, and all he does is read it to you.

The narrator is continuously speaking in every person's head. These people spend their whole life working on their story. They want to have a story worth telling, so they go on adventures like climbing Mount Everest. That mountain has become a great place to observe the collective obsession with story.

"Let me tell you my story as I climbed that mountain," they say.

"Wow. What a great story! I want to have that story to tell, too!" you reply.

There is nothing wrong with climbing mountains. Just don't do it to enhance the worth of your story, but because you enjoy the climbing. Everything else increases the madness on our planet.

It seems as if more and more people get depressed. Is there a way out?

Depression has become a widespread disease, just because people identify themselves with their inner narrator. Your narrator can send you from a happy state into a state of depression in a matter of seconds. All you need to do for that to happen is to listen and believe what it is telling you.

It may be just one thought, or one person you see and that can make your story so heavy that you don't want to carry it around any longer. The only way you can think of to get rid of the story is to dissolve your physical form, to commit suicide.

"This is the only way out of your story," your inner narrator tells you.

You don't need to dissolve your physical form to get rid of the story. In fact, suicide just transfers your story of suffering to other human beings. All you require to dissolve the story is to become aware that the narrator is not who you are.

The more you practice that, the more the brain structure on which your heavy story is running will dissolve. That's the only way to timeless liberation from your story and your worry. That creates new space for enjoyment, love, beauty, abundance and creative spirit to enter.

How can I turn off the inner narrator when it has been there inside my head for most of my life and keeps me awake at night?

The first step is to become aware that the inner narrator is there in your head. It's not bad, it just is there. If you can't recognize it in yourself, then your first step is to write down your self-talk and you'll see the story repeating itself over and over every day.

Once you become aware of the voice in your head, you have a choice to not follow every thought that arises in your mind, but just observe it. Then you're able to see how this voice cuts the world into pieces through words, labels, definitions, interpretations, judgments, comparison, complaining, criticism.

Your attention is the fuel for your voice and the continuous stream of thinking.

So, the second step is to redirect your attention from your head into your body. The best way to do that is through your senses. Through hearing, seeing, smelling, tasting, and touching.

The more you perceive without interpretation, the deeper you enter the present moment and the more peaceful you become.

Are you still breathing?

So, let's take few seconds and turn off the inner narrator by taking three conscious breaths. Bring all your attention to your lips and notice the feeling that the air produces as it touches your lips. Let's take those three breaths now...1...2...3...

See? No mind, no voice in the head, no problem.

Start to integrate a few gaps of "no mind" and "no voice in the head" into your daily life through breathing or performing all your daily activities in full awareness of your senses, like when you brush your teeth, floss, prepare your meals and wash the dishes.

And put something natural, like a plant or flower beside your screen on your work desk and take a few seconds throughout the day to perceive the plant or flower in full awareness of your senses without labeling or judging it.

The more you practice that, the larger the gaps of no mind, no voice in the head become.

That's what "spiritual growth" really is:

"I am <------{spiritual growth}-------> the voice."

The growth away from the voice inside your head.

Jesus called it "salvation". In Hinduism and Yoga it's called "enlightenment". Buddha called it "the end of suffering." I call it "unlimited freedom".

Who will liberate the world from the collective obsession with story?

Stories can be a practical way to convey wisdom, but are the false way to tell you who you are.

The "fault in our stories" manifests in suicide, murder, wars, torture, violence, rape, and shootings. It has claimed over 160 million lives in the past century through warfare and 1 million each year through suicide.

With today's technology, one false story, if it is believed in, could kill that amount in one day. As long as the human obsession with story continues, our species is living at the edge of extinction every day.

Walking through the forest makes you feel so at peace, because there is no story between you and the trees.

The story is the content of our prison cell and the thoughts are the bars that keep us trapped.

The world will be liberated by people who are free from their stories.

You will.

∞

the healer of the madness

I have no money. I have no friends. I have no job. I have no house. I have no spouse. I am unhappy.

"If I were in your situation, I would be unhappy. I would pursue happiness," the world may tell you.

First ask yourself, "Why does not having these things make me unhappy? And how do I know that having these things will make me happy? What if they don't?"

You feel separate from happiness and believe that you need to achieve something first to become happy, as if you could add "happiness" to your life.

Then you start to pursue happiness, and go after the things the world told you will make you happy. But they never do. At the end of your life, you realize that the "pursuit of happiness" was a lie.

You see a rainbow. It makes you feel good. You want to add the rainbow to your life. You start to run towards it. But you never reach it, because it's an illusion created by your mind. This makes you unhappy.

You stop running as you realize that both happiness and unhappiness stem from the same illusion. You close your eyes and feel peace, joy, love, beauty and gratitude. You didn't add these things to you. They have been there inside of you all your life. They are your true nature.

You have woken up out of your dream, entered the awakened life and realized that pursuing happiness is a form of madness.

What do you mean by "madness"?

"Madness" or "insanity" is not a label to judge, but a word that is used for the dysfunctional part of your mind also called "the ego" or "the egoic mind", which is the same as "the fault in our stories".

The ego isn't good or bad. It's just the thing inside you that craves identification and separation. That constant craving is the root of all your unhappiness. "Unhappiness" is the manifestation of the collective madness inside you, hence it is not your personal fault that you feel unhappy.

How do you know that there is a collective madness?

"Food" has become "diet". "Movement" has become "exercise". "Beauty" has become "sexy". "Creation" has become "competition". "Success" has become "money". "Failure" has become "depression". "Leadership" has become "politics". "Security" has become "surveillance". "Peace" has become "ceasefire". "Spirituality" has become "religion". "God" has become "Truth".

What was once normal has become insane. The meaning of the word "normal" has changed. That is the sign that the collective mind has become mad.

Isn't "losing your mind" the same as madness?

In our world, when you "lose your mind", what people mean is that you are completely lost in your thoughts. That's when they call you insane. If that is what insanity means, then 99,999 out of 100,000 people around you are insane, because they're completely lost in their thoughts.

If we take the expression "losing your mind" literally, it would be the best thing that could happen to you, because it means losing the identification with it.

Once you have lost your mind, you have become conscious of your own insanity, and you have become sane.

But when I lose my thoughts, don't I become dumb?

Neuroscientists say that the default state of the brain is that of thinking.

During 16 wakeful hours, the average mind produces about one thought per second. That's nearly 60,000 thoughts each day.

"A person with so many thoughts must be very intelligent," you wonder.

But 99.99% of these thoughts are the same as the day before. Only six thoughts are new each day. Now, reconsider your judgement.

Imagine a person who has reduced the amount of thinking by 90% to one new thought every 10 seconds, a total of 6,000 thoughts each day. But now, just 90% of his thoughts are the same, and 600 are new each day.

"Wow!" you might say, "that person is 100 times smarter even though he or she thinks less."

Knowing how to stop thinking is the secret to happiness and the secret to becoming a more creative person.

You don't have to think as much as you think.

Don't we need thinking to solve the complex problems of humanity?

The human mind makes all problems complex and difficult while all our challenges are simple:

Give hungry people food.

Give homeless people shelter.

Give sick people caring.

Give thirsty people water.

Give poor people a job.

Give young people a future.

Give old people a hand.

Give sad people a smile.

Give cold people warmth.

Give lonely people a hug.

Give fearful people a word.

Give all people love.

Pick one challenge a month and in a year you'll have saved the world. But while you save the world, your priority remains your awakening.

What heals the collective madness?

If you would put a hot iron into the space of the universe, it will lose its energy until it reaches a point just above absolute zero, which is the temperature of the universe itself.

It's the same with a thinking human being. You put it in silence, and it will finally reach the state of silence itself, because that is your natural state.

It's not absolute nothingness, but just above absolute zero.

It's the awareness that is left, and that is the healer of the collective madness.

∞

the awakening academy

Are laws the truth?

Laws are practical, but arbitrary, based on what the collective mind believes is right at the moment. Since laws are not a representation of any form of truth, they can be and are changed, so that they align with the collective identity of the members of their country.

The Chinese identify themselves as people who eat dogs. In Germany this identity is labeled as "abnormal" by law. This happened because the dog became more attached to the identity of the Germans, thus became humanized by the collective mind. If people started to attach themselves to chickens, eating chicken would become "abnormal" by law.

The key is that the term "law" implies that it is derived from a collective belief system like a government or religion.

If a person is more identified with a religion, it will take breaking governmental laws into account in order to enforce the religious laws. This is not the fault of the individual, but the fault in our stories - a manifestation of the identification with the voice in the head.

Becoming free from laws doesn't mean you suddenly drive 80 miles per hour instead of the limit of 40. Accept the laws, but don't make them part of your identity. The function of laws is not to make others wrong and you right. Laws are a tool. Laws are not the Truth.

If you create laws, make sure they serve the whole, not just yourself. Self-serving laws make no sense. If your law fills your pockets, but empties the hearts of your people, you act against a law of nature that can't be broken:

Serve with your whole heart or you create a hole in all hearts - including yours.

What is the function of laws?

Laws have replaced trust.

First, as children, we are taught follow the rules and not our own nature. As adults, we're taught to follow the rules and not trust other people's natures. It's no surprise that humanity has lost trust in itself.

Even the people who give you your forms of communications don't trust you. Each email gets checked, each phone call inspected, and each street corner recorded.

Surveillance has become the government's dragnet. You can escape it only when you're a baby; after that you are trapped inside the net. Whenever they want, they can pull the line and you're forced to the surface where they can just grab you by hand.

Laws are practical to prevent and protect humanity from its own madness, but it seems as if the number and nature of some laws have been fueled by a collective insecurity.

Insecurity is what's left when all trust is lost.

Before people become criminal, they are often good citizens. Why is that?

The criminal potential of a person is directly proportionate to the degree of that person's identification with his or her inner narrator.

No matter how "good" and decent an individual appears to be, if that individual is completely identified with his or her inner narrator, he or she is absolutely capable of cruelties that surpass your imagination. Such an individual would be able to kill a hundred children, one by one without a second thought, if it is what the inner narrator made him or her believe is right.

There have been many examples in history and in today's world of this kind.

"This will never happen again. The people who did these things were different from me," your narrator wants you to believe.

But the people who committed these crimes had the same dysfunctional narrator inside them. It's not their fault. Their narrators have been manipulated by other narrators.

"It wasn't me," they tell you and they are right, because they acted as if they were blind.

The killer that we think is in front of our eyes, is in reality and literally behind our own eyes: the inner narrator.

It seems that prison doesn't make people "better". They often become criminals again. How could we prevent that?

A person robs his neighbors and gets caught.

"I just carried out what the voice in my head was telling me," he assures the judge.

"I just carry out what the law is telling me. It tells me to send you to prison for four years," the judge tells him.

"But you should imprison the devil in my ear, not me," the robber pleads.

"Well, that's what I am going to do. But, your inner narrator still has a strong tie to you, so I have to jail you both," the judge responds.

Solely when that person leaves the prison without the devil in his or her ear, will he or she contribute to the sanity of humanity.

More laws or years don't make people better. Prisons must become an academy for helping people wake up out of their story, because that is the only way to make people "better".

Only once they recognize, "I am not the voice", will they have a choice.

That would be the end of crime on earth.

∞

is this how the world is?

The world is evil. Don't you read the news?

Most "news" are not actually new. They are just new manifestations of the same unconsciousness.

The news are stories created mostly by unconscious humans about other unconscious humans. Hence you will find the same patterns repeated in the headlines every day.

If your sister gave birth to a baby, that is true news. But if your sister hits a parked car, it's nothing new. Just another manifestation of the collective unconsciousness.

Then, what is the benefit of the news?

The most important benefit of the news today: making the unconsciousness obvious.

You come from another planet and you meet a local earthling.

"What is your planet like? What's going on?" you

ask.

"Here are the newspapers from today. Look in the section called 'world news'," the earthling responds.

"Man shoots baby. Poison in the river. Homeless tortured. Dust Lady of 9/11 dead. Mummy will not be relocated. Retired 82-year-old drives 32km in wrong direction. Firefighter in Russia killed by a tree. Fare dodger lies to ticket inspector. Poll shows more depressed people willing to seek help. Two-timers sue online adultery platform. Two colleagues killed during live broadcast," you read.

"What does 9/11 stand for?" you ask.

"The day two planes crashed into two very high buildings and claimed 3,000 lives," the earthling tells you.

"I guess this is a special issue. Please give me the other six issues for this week," you ask.

"Okay," he responds and hands the other six newspapers over to you.

After you've read the "world news" section of each you say, "This must have been a special week."

"No. Not at all. It's quite normal. This is how our world is," he responds.

"What is normal to you seems quite insane to me!" you say.

Why do so many people believe the world is evil?

A farmer in Germany opens his smartphone in the morning and reads that ten children have been shot 4,000 miles away from him. The shooter was a child too.

The distance doesn't matter to the mind. It still gets its daily proof of "this is how the world is".

Since eighty percent of the news is negative, the collective mind started to believe that the world is bad and that people are evil by nature. Through that lens, it sees only evil. It's not that people have become bad, it's the collective mind that has become mad.

Imagine a world in peace and without violence. Nothing negative happens beyond your doorstep. You would not have to worry about terrorists, nuclear wars or your neighbor.

Would you still read the news in such a paradise?

Should I read the news or not?

Your state of consciousness is more important than whether you read the news or not. The news can be useful if you want to plan to go to a country where there is a lot of violence. Or you should not drink the tap water anymore, because something got spilled into it.

But if you perceive the news in awareness, then there is no identification with it, like "This is how the world is now."

Is the increasing madness a bad thing?

No. If the human mind hadn't become increasingly dysfunctional it would have remained unnoticed. The madness is the very thing that allows the awakening to accelerate. We must be grateful for it, not resent it.

Don't start your days with nurturing your inner narrator through the news, but start your day by nurturing your Being through a glass of water, a prayer, a smile, a conscious breath. That is how you make your sanity obvious.

You don't need to know more about the world than that.

∞

the unbelievable truth

How can I be free? This is the only truth. Don't you see!?

There is the Truth that is absolute and a "truth" that is learned. Let me explain.

You have just heard a new thought. You carve it into a piece of wood. The new thought has become your new idea.

You hear the new idea again. You take your carving tool and trace the new idea on the wood. The groove gets deeper and the new idea has become your new opinion.

You hear the new opinion again. You take your carving tool and trace the new opinion on the wood. The groove gets deeper and the new opinion has become your new belief.

You hear the new belief again. You take your carving tool and trace the new belief on the wood. The groove gets deeper and the new belief has become your new conviction.

You hear the new conviction again. You take your carving tool and trace the new conviction on the wood. The groove gets deeper and the new conviction has become your new "truth".

Burn the wood and you are free.

How do I know whether I have found the Truth or a "truth"?

The depth of the groove determines how much you have identified yourself with the original thought. When someone questions your "truth", you feel as if you're defending your very life and get angry.

When someone questions the Truth, you become more peaceful. This is how you know whether you've found the Truth or a "truth".

Are you angry or peaceful now?

Where does a "truth" come from?

Most opinions that people have, have taken form in their brain structures through repetitive conditioning by TV, media, and news.

Continuous exposure to an idea or a thought

connects certain brain cells and creates a neurocircuit. That neurocircuit is like a groove in your wood. With every repetition this neurocircuit gets strengthened and the idea becomes more true for you. Finally, it becomes a belief or even a conviction.

The only physiological difference between an opinion, belief, conviction, and "truth" is the amount and strength of the neurons that are connected in your brain. "Truth", here, of course, means conditioned truth that a person adopts as absolute.

The stronger the neuron is, the thicker the neural connections are and the stronger your belief is. The stronger the belief is, the stronger the emotion you feel when someone questions that belief.

Sense experiences serve as triggers that activate a neurocircuit. Somewhere in your brain, there is a neurocircuit that represents your name. That circuit lights up whenever you read, hear, or see your name, because your name is the trigger for that circuit.

Whenever a person wants your attention, all they

need to do is to call your name.

This sounds scientific. Isn't science the truth?

You are sitting in the shadow of an apple tree.

You look up and admire the delicious apple that hangs there above your head. Before you reach out to grab it, it falls down right on your forehead.

"What was the invisible hand that pulled the apple down onto my head before I could?" you wonder.

You spend the rest of your afternoon sitting below the apple tree contemplating this question.

It's starting to get dark. The sky is clear. You look up into the eternal blueness to inspire your creative source. There you see it. A white disk. Actually three quarters of a white disk.

"It's the moon," they've told you.

For one second, all your thoughts vanish, and all your perceptions and conditioned beliefs are gone. There is peace in your mind and body like you never experienced it before.

Then out of the blue, a thought reaches the surface of your mind, "What if the invisible hand that pulls the moon towards the earth is the same that pulled the apple down onto my forehead?"

This thought gives you goosebumps. You develop mathematics and derive equations to support your realization. You develop a new science that points to this truth.

I tell you this little story because it displays what most people, even established scientists, get wrong when they hear or speak about science. They believe "Science" is the same as "Truth." But science changes, gets reinvented and readjusted. The Truth never changes.

No matter how complex, mathematical or how much evidence you have for your theory of truth, you will never be able to describe the truth perfectly, through thoughts, words or numbers. You can, however, experience it perfectly. That's what happened when the apple hit your forehead.

Isn't science the way to understand who I am?

You don't need a bundle of thoughts to "know"

something. You can know without understanding it. Science can never tell you who you are, but you can experience it when you take a breath.

Identification with a theory will give you a sense of certainty that you understand how the world is, until someone else comes along and proves your theory wrong. A theory is a theory until it's proven wrong. Then it has become a lie.

Science is a tool, not the truth. Do it because you enjoy the doing, not because you like to identify with your theory or the role of being a scientist.

Physicists thought they'd found the atom, but then they found even smaller particles inside the atoms, called "quarks".

They spend billions of dollars to look further and further into the form and what they will ultimately find is the formless essence.

That's when they will have found themselves.

No matter matters.

This sounds spiritual. Isn't religion about the truth?

You have found an old cake recipe from your great-great-grandmother.

You send an email to your best friend. "Hey, I've found an old recipe for a cake. It's easy. All the measurements are in cups. I've invited eight of our friends tomorrow for cake. Could you also bake one? You'll find the recipe attached to this email. Have fun. See you tomorrow at 3pm."

The next day you sit with your best friend and eight other friends at the kitchen table with two cakes in front of you.

You watch your eight other friends munch on the cake. Then one of them says, "I like this one the most." The other friend says, "Well, to me the other is better." You take a bite of the other cake and indeed it tastes different.

After your friends are gone, you sit on your balcony looking at the tree in front of you and wonder, "How is it possible that both cakes tasted different even though they were baked from exactly the same recipe?"

For one hour you sit there, but find no answer. Then suddenly it appears. "The size of the cup she used for the ingredients must have been different from mine!"

What does this story have to do with religion?

All religions are baked from the same recipe, but every religion uses their own cups. None is better than the other, they just taste different. Choose the one you like. If you don't like cakes. That's also fine.

Out of one universal Truth became a whole system of relative beliefs - stories about the Truth. One person interprets something, creates a new story and his or her followers adopt this relative belief into their belief system. Then, the followers change the label from "relative" belief to "absolute". They have carved a new "truth" into their wood.

That's why even the people who seek to become more spiritual often become more insane once they join a religion. Again, "insanity" is nothing bad. And no religion is bad.

Some followers of a religion believe that the thoughts that have been presented to them by a preacher, a book or a sermon are the same as "Truth". These people will tell you that when you join you can also make it part of your identity.

If your story and their story about the Truth do not match up, they feel very separate from you. They will argue that you are wrong and justify their story of the Truth, "So and so spoke these words a few thousand years ago. The story about that has been sold a billion times."

The age of a story and the number of people who tell it, are a sign of how deeply a "truth" has been conditioned into the collective unconsciousness. Hence, the story appears very "true" to the members of that very collective unconsciousness.

If you meet such a person, never argue with them or tell them they are wrong as they will get angry and violent. A core belief - a "truth" - makes people blind, and they may feel justified to inflict harm upon you.

Walk away from such people in a peaceful manner or turn the interaction into a spiritual practice of non-judgment and non-reaction.

Doesn't having a religion make me more spiritual?

Having a belief system like a religion, does not make you a spiritual person. The more you identify with that belief system, as it gives you a sense of who you are, the greater the gap between you and spirituality becomes.

How spiritual you are depends on only one thing: your connectedness to this moment.

Now I am confused. Does God exist or not?

You can't find God in the outside world or in Heaven. You can search inside yourself and still you won't find it. It's not because it isn't there. It's because it's you. You are God.

There are many words to describe that like Soul, Source, Life, Love, Tao, Universe, Space, Awareness, Consciousness, Presence, the Now, Stillness, the Formless, Truth - all the words point to the same essence. Your essence is that.

That's why you can't find God in the realm of your mind. You can only experience it. To find God, all you need is to go beyond the story, not necessarily go into a church. Although this is a great place to feel your essence in the silence that the church provides.

The true God knows no fears and has no enemies. You can only be afraid of loss of form and an enemy of a form. The formless doesn't know loss or enemies. It knows only oneness and eternity. It knows that nothing is ever lost or separate.

Everything the universe contains has always been there and will always remain there. Even you, the God, the consciousness that you are, is eternal.

It's not a question of whether there is evidence in the dimension of form to prove that God exists or not. Just by being conscious of your own consciousness, you are the evidence.

If science and religion are not the Truth, then spirituality must be it!?

You are right, science or religion are not the Truth. Both are merely one way to understand the world - ways of the mind.

But even spirituality is not the Truth, just another way to understand the world - the way without the mind.

And that is your way to save us.

What is the absolute Truth?

It is the ocean in which your thoughts arise.

It is the paper on which your words appear.

It is one with humankind.

It is who you are.

∞

the gap of separation

What is "the gap of separation"?

You stand on firm ground. In front of you is another human being so close that this person's toes touch yours. You can see yourself in this person as if your toes were touching a mirror.

Then you ask this human being his or her name. The person responds and suddenly you hear a cracking sound. You look down to your feet and notice a ten-centimeter rift between your toes and the toes of the other human being.

You continue asking about age, profession, food, country, culture, tribe, family, friends, beliefs, possessions, native language. With each response, the rift between you both widens and the other human being gets farther away from you.

Finally, "the gap of separation" as I call it, has expanded to the horizon and you can't see the other human anymore. Now, you can point your gun at this tiny speck on the horizon and shoot. It won't affect you. You won't even hear this human being's scream.

There are men and women. Isn't that a natural gap of separation? How can they be the same?

Your body determines the story of your gender.

Most human beings are completely identified with that story and act it out in the role of "man" or "woman". Men think they are very separate from women, and do everything they can to prove that to the world. Women do the same. This creates a gap of separation within the same species.

It's true that the psychological and physiological forms of men and women are different, but the One Life that animates their bodies is the same for both.

In my neighborhood are people with a different skin color and I don't speak their language. How can we be the same?

If you travel to a foreign country, it's very easy to believe that you are separate from the people who live there. Their culture is different. Their food tastes different. Their skin color is different.

You don't speak their language and you think that this is a barrier for understanding. But, when you interact without the narrator in your head, you'll notice that their tone of voice, the look in their eyes and their body language give you more than you need to understand each other.

Interacting with a person with whom you share no language and no story can be liberating not limiting.

In your head you may call this person "foreigner", because he or she appears to be different. But in your heart you might as well call this person by your very name, because beyond your story, you are both the same.

How can I label a person so that I don't fall in the trap that this person is separate from me?

"This person's name is such and such. She does such and such. She has such and such. Therefore she is such a person," they say.

The deeper way to describe another human being is by their presence. Yes, call this human being "presence", not "person". You can label this presence by using a name for practical purposes. But by labeling a presence rather than a person, the essence of the human being is not disguised.

Then, you'll never fall into the trap of the narrator in your head that tells you that you are separate from this person.

How do I know that I've closed the gap of separation?

Humans have created a jigsaw puzzle of the world. They have largely separated each piece to examine it, and as a result, lost the picture of the whole. But science has proven what we already know in our hearts:

We come from the same source. All the atoms in our bodies evolved from a single point, called the "Space-Time Singularity". From that point, the universe expanded.

We all have the same age, 13.8 billion years. That's the age of the universe, and therefore the age of all of us. If you believe that is too old for you, let's take 4.6 billion years. That is the age of the solar system.

We are all made of the same stuff. All our atoms come from the same galactic cloud that also formed the sun, the earth, all the planets and moons in our solar system. Some elements in our bodies were created during the birth of the universe, some during the death of stars.

We all share the same ancestors. There was a single place from which we all migrated, called "The Cradle of Humankind". There was a single mother that the entire living world population comes from, named "Mitochondrial Eve".

We are one species. What causes the most suffering on this planet is the belief that we are separate from a human being with a different skin color, language, culture, sex, religion and so on.

These barriers have been created by our heads. In our hearts we have known all along that we are one. Closing the Gap of Separation is a testament to both our singularity and our humanity.

It's in a moment of compassion that you know that you've closed that gap.

∞

the war of the minds

I am the leader of an army and all I want is to create a better world for my people. Don't I have the right to live in a paradise?

First, understand that there is "paradise" and Paradise; "paradise" is learned, like "truth". You may have learned it from a book that says, "This is the promised land. This is how paradise looks."

The true Paradise cannot be found in a book. It can only be found inside you right next to Peace and Truth. In fact, they are all in the same place.

Your vision of "a better world" in the future will destroy us. The world cannot become a "paradise" in the future. There will never be a better world than the one you stand upon.

Hitler's vision of a "paradise" claimed over 80 million lives. That is about the total population of Germany today. This means for each person who lives in Germany, one person has been killed during World War II. That could only happen because Hitler and the population were completely identified with the voice inside their head.

If you try to build your "paradise" through the enslavement, torture and murder of people, all fruits that grow in your "paradise" will taste bitter. Do you want to live in such a land?

Often, people kill because they seek "paradise" not on earth, but in Heaven. You desperately stretch your hands towards that Heaven, not realizing that it's merely hot air painted by your mind - a fata morgana.

Instead of projecting the "paradise" into the sky, why not seek true Paradise on the soil you stand upon? What is the worth of all the affluence in Heaven when the price you pay for this is the future of your children?

If you kill for the "paradise" in Heaven, you create Hell on earth. If you find Paradise inside of you, you create heaven on earth.

But I have to fill the world with my truth. Don't you see the falsehood in the world?

You have just adopted a "truth" as the absolute Truth. Underneath your deep commitment to this one "truth", you can already sense a fear that this is not the absolute Truth in the universe. If it were the absolute Truth, then it would be in every human already and you wouldn't have to convince people of it through force.

That other people don't want to accept your truth makes you angry and you feel very separate from them. You feel they are wrong and you are right.

Don't I have the right to be right?

There is a road near my home which is unusually narrow. When two cars approach each other, both have to veer a little onto the side stripe. If neither of the two drivers complies, both crash.

One person claims his or her right to be right. The other tries to claim back the right to be right through force. When two people want to be right, both are wrong.

Be kind and you're always right.

Are you telling me that I am wrong?

No. I am not here to question your beliefs. All I do is tell you that the people you call "infidels" or "apostates" experience exactly the same feelings inside them as you.

They feel hurt and angry too, because you tell them "I have the absolute truth and you have a lie." They believe you are the liar.

If a dog believes it's a cat, because it has been raised by cats, it is still a dog, don't you agree? Would you beat the dog because it believes it is a cat? Why not let the dog believe that it is a cat if this is what makes the dog happy?

Or are you afraid of cats?

But I know that my truth is the only absolute truth in this world. It's as true to me as the fact that my name is my name.

You tell someone your name and that person responds, "I don't believe you."

You would get disturbed or even angry, because your name has been imprinted deeply not only in your brain, but also on your identity card.

In its essence, your name is a "truth". You believe that this is your name. A name can be a practical tool to organize and get your attention. It should be used as such, not to define who you are.

If each of us thinks his or her truth is absolute, we will become a planet of gravestones. If each of us thinks his or her truth is relative, we will become a planet of bright stars.

Time is relative to the observer, but absolute to those who look at the same watch. It's the same with "truth".

Once you no longer get angry when someone questions what you believe, you know the absolute Truth.

How should I treat a "terrorist" if I meet one?

Not like a terrorist.

If you treat people like terrorists, you enhance their sense of identity and only make them worse. If you treat them with respect, like soldiers of a "truth" who defend their beliefs, you may promote them upwards and away from their own self-image of being terrorists.

Hence, they may recognize their own humanity

again. It doesn't mean they will, but the chance is much greater.

You call him "terrorist" and he calls you a "terrorist". Who is right? Both and none.

Is a terrorist is a bad person?

What is worse: 100 people who are killed in a terrorist attack or 100 people who are killed in a company explosion?

None.

The fact is, both events are equally tragic and can't be undone. The only difference is the meaning these events have in your head.

That meaning is created as the inner narrator interprets both events based on your past conditioning. It is likely that you have accumulated negative opinions towards people who are labeled as "terrorists" through what you heard or saw about them. That is why you feel a much stronger response to the terrorist attack.

Emotion is what sells the newspaper, not information. Hence, you'll find a terrorist attack on the front page, while the company explosion will be buried in the middle section or not mentioned at all.

The terrorist is just bad in your head. This doesn't mean it's okay what he or she is doing. It means that it's no reason to store resentment or anger inside you towards what we call "terrorists".

My goal is not to make anyone wrong, but to clear your head and raise the quality of your actions.

How can we create world peace?

First, understand that there is Peace and "peace"; "peace" is like pleasure. It's transient.

Often, people think they need to be at war to be at peace with themselves. As a soldier, you earn most of your honor in war. As an arms manufacturer, you earn most of your money in war. Without war, lots of people would lose their jobs. It seems as if "peace" and occasional war is the only option that makes economic sense.

There are soldiers who have awakened during their call of duty. In the midst of Hell, they have found Heaven. They saw the futility in their deeds. They realized that every hole they leave in their enemies leaves a hole in their heart as well. Upon their return, they've become messengers of Peace to heal that hole.

How will we know that we have world Peace rather than world "peace"?

As long as there are weapons there will only be "peace" - which has become another word for ceasefire. This means that the majority of people are not at Peace with themselves and the world. They think they need to protect "peace". But true Peace needs no protection.

Humans will look back at this age as we look back at the Medieval period. We will walk into a museum and marvel at the cleverly thought out weapons we once developed to kill and torture each other. The ingenuity of human insanity will make us chuckle.

Why chuckle?

It's better to laugh at our own madness than to cry. Too many tears have already been shed. There was a time for madness. There was a time for sadness. Now is the time for gladness.

Who are we really fighting against?

Let's go back a few million years...

The world's first family of human ancestors is living in a cave by a river. Soon, their offspring create the world's second family, who move into a cave on the other riverbank.

"This is now my country, and that is yours. The river is our border. You must never cross it without my permission," the head of one family says.

In few years, a certain fruit has become scarce on one side of the river while it has become abundant on the other side. For practical purposes we label one country's members the "Scarcers" and the others the "Abundants".

The head of the Scarcers asks for permission to cross the river. "May I come over to your place to take a walk and admire your country?"

"If this is all you request, you shall be welcome," the head of the Abundants replies.

The Scarcer crosses the river. While he is walking in the Abundant country he is picking some of the fruits that are scarce in his country and puts them in a bag around his neck.

Then the Scarcer returns to the river. "Your country is a paradise."

"Thank you. I am glad you enjoyed it. May I see your bag?" he requests.

"Yes, of course," he says and hands over the bag of fruit.

The Abundant looks into the bag and suddenly his face becomes angry.

"I welcomed you into my country and you exploited it behind my back. You shall pay the price of these fruits with your life." the head of the Abundants shouts.

Then he orders his family members to tie a stone on the feet of the traitor and throw him in the river for every one of the Scarcers to see as a warning.

The Scarcers are outraged by such a cruel deed from their former family members. "From now on you are no longer members of our family, but we shall be enemies and we will seek revenge upon you."

The very first world war was declared. All other wars that happened in human history, are happening, or will ever happen are offspring of this first world war that started few millions years ago.

Since all living human beings come from the same mother called "Mitochondrial Eve", all wars are merely family disputes.

How can two family members kill each other when they have been living in peace for all these years?

Hitler created metaphors and symbols to give people an identity. Then he tweaked the collective identity of his enemies to maximize the gap of separation between the German population and the Jews. This gap became so wide that people couldn't see any connection anymore. Hence they could kill a Jew without a second thought.

This is the recurring pattern in all conflicts that involve mass killings of ordinary people within a population. The leaders of the active force give their followers a central symbol, core beliefs to identify with and increase the separateness of themselves from the enemies in the minds of their followers through extensive propaganda tactics. Then killing becomes a commodity.

Even two neighbors who have been living in peace for 30 years, shared their vegetables and invited each other for dinner, could kill each other from one day to the next, just because they have two core beliefs - stories about the truth - that produce a large gap of separation in their minds.

Now, you can understand the genocide in Rwanda and why "Auschwitz" is still happening...

Why do the eyes of people who commit these crimes look so empty?

People who are possessed by their story run around with empty eyes, because the essence of who they are cannot shine through the shell of their story. They are blind.

The peacemaker and the warlord are blinded by their story, and hence both create more suffering than they are able to reduce.

What is the common root of all these wars?

A few million years ago all continents were one.

The belief that "this is the border of my country, you may not question it" is the collective inner narrator. It wants to feel significant because it can say that to you. It wants to feel separate so it divided the planet into countries, and the human species into nationalities.

A few thousand years ago all religions were one.

The belief "this is the absolute truth, you may not question it" is the collective inner narrator. It wants to feel separate so it divided the Truth into religions, and the human species into believers and infidels.

The questioning of a belief triggers a stream of thinking in your mind. The thoughts take form as emotions in your body. Emotions become the behaviors that are defending the belief.

All wars are mind-made since they are all induced by questioning beliefs.

To protect the gap of separation and the sense of

identity, the mind uses war. It's not people who kill. It's not weapons that kill. It's not people who pull the trigger. It's the mind that kills. Every war in the past, present and future, has been, is, and will always be, a war of the minds.

It's the most destructive manifestation of the collective dysfunction - the fault in our stories. It's a bug in the operating system that runs the brain.

Again, it's caused by one delusion: selling relative truth as absolute truth.

And the common root of all wars is the inner narrator.

I am a president. How can there be eternal Peace without war? Don't we have to protect ourselves and other nations?

There are situations when we have to protect ourselves against the collective insanity. But we must be careful that through our defense we don't make ourselves part of the insanity. At the moment, we do.

Peace created through warfare will always cycle back to war. With each cycle the collective inner narrator on both sides becomes more mad until it bursts. Suffering created in this way is timeless.

No mind, no war.

To create peace through war leads to eternal war. To create peace through liberation from the mind leads to eternal peace.

There has never been an "awakened" president in world history.

Will you be our first one?

∞

part 3

your next step

Whenever a species gets close to extinction,
we put it on the Red List. If we don't wake up,
we will have to put ourselves on that list
in a few hundred years.

- *Fabian*

awakening the new species

I guess you've noticed it: the world has become increasingly insane.

I guess you are sensing it: if the human madness continues at its current pace, we won't survive another thousand years.

I guess you've learned it: when the old species is no longer capable of survival, the next step in its evolution becomes a must.

What is the next step?

It's not: to migrate to Mars.

It's not: to become plant eaters.

It's not: to find the world formula.

The next step is to become free from the voice in your head.

The more I see the world become insane, the more peaceful I become, because the more I know that humanity is becoming ready to take this step.

Human history, so far, is a story of madness. Whether the story of our species will be titled The Tragedy of Humanity or The Triumph of Humanity depends on your next step.

Transform or die?

These are the choices a caterpillar has. Human beings who are possessed by their minds are like caterpillars.

To survive, we don't have to become better at crawling or thinking, but we have to transcend our mind-made cocoon and rise into the realm of the formless.

Awakening is the most essential evolvement in the history of the human species. It is a silent movement and you won't find it in the news. The madness is much louder. But ultimately, the destiny of each sound is stillness.

What are some of the characteristics of the new species?

It sees itself in every human being, and others can see themselves in it because it has let go of the story you call "self-image".

It is able to look at things and other beings in full awareness without the need to judge, interpret or label them.

It allows people to be, doesn't become angry and reactive when they don't follow the mind-made rules.

Its behavior is no longer a result of conditioned reactions, but conscious choices.

It is resilient to stress, because it is able to fully accept whatever the content of the present moment is.

It has escaped the vicious cycle of negative thinking and depression, worry, fear, anxiety, and panic are no longer part of its daily life.

It lives an honest, gentle and inspired life, where all it does is trusting in its guidance and following its intuition.

It is free from the fear of death, because it knows who it is beyond the body and its personal history.

Its internal state of being no longer depends on what's happening in the outside world.

It never forces awakening upon others, because it knows its responsibility is only for its own state of consciousness. By cultivating this state in itself, it cultivates this state in others without doing or wanting anything from them.

It doesn't see itself as "a new species", but as a healer of the Gap of Separation, because it recognizes the new species in every human on earth.

Imagine a world in which human beings have evolved into their highest form.

Evolving into your highest form means becoming who you are, which is all you can be, which is formless. Yes, your highest form is formless.

If just for one second all humankind would escape their negative thought patterns and become one with the present moment, the world would cease to be dysfunctional, cease to fight, and be united by the Now.

It doesn't require time to reach a state of eternal

peace. Let's take one conscious breath now and create world peace for a second.

Is it important to save the human species?

In a few billion years the Sun will turn the Earth into a piece of coal. Humankind is working very hard to achieve it within a thousand years.

In the era in which these words are written, the sun is providing us with the perfect energy to survive and thrive. A little less, and we would be frozen. A little more, and we would evaporate.

This is the perfect era for our species. Most people believe that this is how it's going to be forever. But, like the human species, stars don't live forever. The length of their lives is determined by their mass.

The sun has already lived for 4.6 billion years. She is in her best years now and has few billion years left to lighten up our sky and to keep our bodies warm.

After that, the sun will enter the autumn of her life and grow into a red giant. She will swallow Mercury, then Venus, then Earth.

The oceans will evaporate. Every house, every invention, every weapon, every book, every story, every idea, every border, every religion, all the money, everything humans ever built will be burned down to ashes. That's when the era of all life forms on earth is over.

From that cosmic perspective, whether humanity will survive the next thousand years doesn't matter.

Saving the human species is urgent, but not important.

What do you mean by "not important"?

"Your peace" is your priority, not "world peace".

Whether your life will be a success doesn't depend on whether you saved the world or not. It only depends on one thing: How connected are you to the answer of "Who am I?"

You can only save us by allowing the new species to awaken within you.

Do you believe that humanity will make it through the next few hundred years?

The collective human mind is the wind that fans the fire of hell. Your awakening is the water that soothes it. Once the amount of water reaches a critical mass, the great fire will end, and our planet will be transformed into a thriving land.

Since you have read till now, I raise my stakes that we will make it.

∞

bye.

What if we'll meet again
in our next life?

- *Fabian*

bye.

Is this all there is?

When I first asked that question, I answered it with "No. It's not all there is. Life must have more in store for me."

So, I started searching for the one thing that would give me fulfillment. I looked for it in girls, in physics, in running, in reading, in my travels, in my family, in food, and in my social circle, but the fulfillment I found never lasted. I was always headed for the next "kick".

The question that seemed so promising in the beginning left me hopeless, frustrated and depressed in the basement of my parents' house at 29.

I slept on the couch, despite having a bed next door. I thought, I am going to move out in a few weeks anyway. There was no reason to get comfortable around here.

There were days when I didn't leave the house and

weeks when I didn't see my father even though we were living in the same building. I didn't sleep well. I felt tired. I wasn't moving my body a lot. I got severe migraines. I went to the doctor at least once a week, because I thought I was going to die.

One day, I took out a piece of paper, titled it "Living after you awakened" and started to write:

Sometimes there are these moments when I wish I would never have awakened. That everything would be back to normal again. That this moment that changed my life had never occurred. Realizing that for all my life I had been identified with and controlled by the voice inside my head shifted my life for good. Nothing's like before.

I don't want to spend as much time with my friends as I used to. Before I drank 10 liters of beer a week, now I haven't had a sip for nearly two years. I haven't had sex for nearly three years, but it doesn't matter much to me. I don't enjoy going out in the evening. For a year I didn't attend any birthday parties and declined all weddings.

It's just hard to be around people who are not awakened yet. Nobody really understands me and they get uncomfortable or even angry when I talk about it. I fear that I will lose all my friends and be left alone.

I feel trapped on my new path. It seems as if I am not making any progress in my life. At nearly 30 years old, I have no job, no money, no girlfriend, no social life, and I live with my parents. And it doesn't feel good to be around people who ask me why I don't have these things.

What am I doing wrong?

You are living in resistance to what is. You resist where you are. You resist how the people around you are. You resist letting go of your attachment to friends and things. Above all, you resist your awakening.

The last sentence was exactly what I needed to hear. I was afraid of the effect that my awakening would have on my life. But I also knew that once the door towards the awakened life has opened you can't close it again and pretend that nothing has happened.

That day, I started to allow the new state of consciousness to flow into my life. Soon I began to experience a life without suffering, without stress, and without fear. A few days afterward, all that unhappiness was nearly gone. I slept better. The migraine attacks reduced. I started to walk and workout regularly. I felt alive again.

Now, I can see clearly how this period in the basement of my parents' house has become the single most important period of my life. This experience has put me on the path I had originally been assigned to when I was born:

To help people make the transition into the awakened life.

The fact that I've written this book doesn't mean that I am a perfectly awakened person. This book is my companion as much as it is yours. One could say it has become a true friend.

This book may have cracked the door open for you. Or, this book may have helped you to cross the doorstep. In the end, this door will open for everyone. So, embrace the doorknob, lift your foot, take a deep breath, and step in.

In your next life, you won't remember any of this. But there is no need to worry about whether you'll become awakened again. You'll have to leave the words behind, but you'll take the Truth with you. I'll remind you of the Truth again. That is my job.

Finally, I've asked the question "Is this all there is?" again, with the slight difference that now the "there" was pointed inward.

"Yes. It is all there is," is my answer.

You no longer need to search for fulfillment outside. It's already in you.

In fact, you are it.

∞

About Fabian, the Writer

Who is Fabian?

"Fabian" died on December 5th, 2013. Now, it's just a name to which things have been attached, like a birth certificate dated January 4th, 1986, a Master's degree in Physics from the University of Heidelberg in 2014, and now this book.

What is your greatest achievement so far? This book?

No. Writing the book was easy. The hardest part, by far, was following the nudge of the universe. Every person on the planet gets this nudge at some point in their lives, but just 1 out of 1,000,000 follows it.

Why is it so hard?

It's because the wind of the world is blowing in the opposite direction. It's tempting to just hoist the sails and start running before the wind. But that's the least effective way of sailing. You'll get more speed once you adjust your course a bit towards the wind. By that you'll automatically adjust the course of your life towards your natural talents.

What is your main goal in life?

What is a goal? It's a thought you have about getting from A to B. Most people confuse goals with purpose.

The goal of driving a car is to get to B. The purpose of driving a car is not to get to B, but to drive the car.

The goal of working out is to improve your health, lose weight or build muscles. The purpose of working out is not improve your health, to lose weight or build muscles, but to work out.

The goal of drinking a glass of water is to satisfy your thirst. The purpose of drinking a glass of water is not to satisfy your thirst, but to drink the water.

The purpose of your life - at any given time - is always the same:

Being aware of what you are doing.

Knowing that purpose at all times is my main goal in life.

thank you ;-)

After I had finished the first draft of this book, I wondered why a writer needs an editor. Now I know. The job of a writer is to give the reader a new perspective - a new window - from which to look at the world. The job of the editor is to clean the window for the reader.

For this book I couldn't have imagined a better editor than Catherine Traffis. She is not only a very talented editor, but also very enjoyable to work with. Her work made this book magical.

Whatever mountain you have chosen to climb, humans have left fixed ropes along their route to make your ascent easier. Learn the ropes and route from them. That's what I did.

Especially, I have to thank Marc Allen. His responses to my questions on Facebook made my ascent much easier.

When you have finished the first chapter of your own book, send it to a person you know, like and trust. This person will give you honest feedback.

To me this person is Regina Huber. I would like to thank her for taking the time to review my very first chapter and for sending me her feedback in the form of a letter.

There may come a point in your life when you realize that the path you've been on for the past few years feels like a lie. Never be ashamed to move in with your parents to restart from scratch - even if you're 30.

My dearest love goes to my parents for giving me the support and trust I needed to write this book. Without you, this book would not have been published yet.

When you look at our modern society, it seems that we have lost respect for our elders. We call our grandmothers "granny." You call her "cute", but what can you learn from her?

"You've chosen a rocky road." My grandmother often told me while pressing a 50 euro note in my hand. At this point, I want to thank my grandmother for her wisdom and support.

Before I started to write this book, I visited the grave of my grandfather where he was buried 10 years ago. Still, to this day, his voice echoes in my ear, "One day, you'll be a doctor." Now, I know he meant "author". I send him love.

Every day I wrote, I went to bed imagining myself as my reader. He or she would read a line from the book, place it on his or her bedside table, close his or her eyes and peacefully fall asleep with a smile.

That's why, finally, I want you, the reader, to know how grateful I am that you made my vision real and invited this book into your life.

I love you.

♥

credits

There may have been some moments while you were reading this book that made you think, "I've read that before" or "I've heard that before". You may even find parts that are exactly written like in another book.

That doesn't mean I've copied and pasted these words into this book. No. The Truth is always the same. Sometimes it just happens that you use the same words to describe it.

There are, however, a few people that I want to mention since they guided me through their work:

Wayne Dyer, Eckhart Tolle, Oprah Winfrey, Kahlil Gibran, Niall Ferguson, Robert Greene, Viktor Frankl, Paulo Coelho, Nelson Mandela, Immaculee Ilibagiza, Tony Robbins, Steve Taylor, Chandler Bolt, James Altucher, Robin Sharma, Joe Dispenza, Daniel Pink, Brendon Burchard, Simon Sinek, Seth Godin, Robert Cialdini, Les Brown, Christiane Stenger, and the greatest guide of all: the universe.

help me.

As a young boy I often wondered "How can I make a difference? I am just a little person. I can't do big things to change the world."

It's true that big things change the world, but they never last and often make things worse. It's really the small things that bring about positive change that endures.

I want you to know how much I appreciate that you took the time to read this book. If you have found some little spelling errors, you can let me know at fm@fabimarkl.com. I'll use your input to make the next version better.

Or, if you just leave a review on Amazon for this book, then in a minuscule way, you'll have positively impacted the whole world.

The book is small. I am small. You are small, but together we will make a big difference.

- Fabian

12924069R00133

Printed in Poland
by Amazon Fulfillment
Poland Sp. z o.o., Wrocław